ONGOING
CRISIS
COMMUNICATION

SAGE SERIES IN PUBLIC RELATIONS

SERIES EDITORS
Robert L. Heath and Gabriel M. Vasquez

Embracing ideas as old as the rhetorical heritage of Western Civilization and as new as theoretical models that draw on social science, the **Sage Series in Public Relations** comprises the work of academics and professional practitioners. Combining theory and practice, authors seek to redefine the field through thoughtful examinations of the breadth and depth of public relations. Books in the series may offer emphasis on theory, research foundations, or practice, but all focus on advancing public relations excellence. The series publishes work devoted to the principle that public relations adds economic, sociopolitical, and cultural value to society, particularly those based on democratic ideals.

Books in this series:

Communication Planning: An Integrated Approach
   Sherry Devereaux Ferguson

Ongoing Crisis Communication: Planning, Managing, and Responding
   W. Timothy Coombs

SSPR
Sage Series in Public Relations

ONGOING CRISIS COMMUNICATION
Planning, Managing, and Responding

W. Timothy Coombs

SAGE Publications
International Educational and Professional Publisher
Thousand Oaks   London   New Delhi

For information:

SAGE Publications, Inc.
2455 Teller Road
Thousand Oaks, California 91320
E-mail: order@sagepub.com

SAGE Publications Ltd.
6 Bonhill Street
London EC2A 4PU
United Kingdom

SAGE Publications India Pvt. Ltd.
M-32 Market
Greater Kailash I
New Delhi 110 048 India

Printed in the United States of America

Library of Congress Cataloging-in-Publication Data

Coombs, W. Timothy
    Ongoing crisis communication: Planning, managing, and responding /
by W. Timothy Coombs
        p. cm. — (Sage series in public relations; v. 2)
    Includes bibliographical references (p.) and index.
    ISBN 0-7619-1319-X (cloth: alk. paper)
    ISBN 0-7619-1320-3 (pbk.: alk. paper)
        1. Crisis management.   2. Communication in management.
    I. Title.   II. Series.
        HD49.C664   1999
        658.4′056—dc21   99-6438

This book is printed on acid-free paper.

99   00   01   02   03   10   9   8   7   6   5   4   3   2   1

Acquiring Editor: Margaret H. Seawell
Editorial Assistant: Renée Piernot
Production Editor: Astrid Virding
Editorial Assistant: Nevair Kabakian
Typesetter: Marion Warren

Contents

Preface

In the early 1980s, I was assigned to read an article about gallows rhetoric—what people said before they were hung. Gallows researchers had found similar patterns in what people said in these speeches. In a moment of inspiration or insanity, I made a connection between gallows rhetoric and how some corporations were handling recent high-profile crises. So my curiosity with crisis communication and crisis management began.

The writings about crisis management prove I am not alone in the desire to understand and improve crisis management. Over the years, I have read many fascinating articles and books on the subject. I use the word *fascinating* because the writings stimulated my thinking about and guided my research into crisis management. More recently, I have been haunted by the fragmented nature of the crisis management literature. Two qualities have created this sense of fragmentation. First, researchers from various disciplines are addressing crisis management but too often ignore similar research in other disciplines. The end result is sometimes duplication and often impoverishment because the additional ideas could have strengthened a line of research. Second, researchers tend to study "parts" of crisis management, not the whole process. Studying parts of crisis management is rewarding if at some point we can step back and see how the various parts fit into the bigger picture.

Integrative efforts are far too rare in crisis management. We see more single-disciplinary work than multidisciplinary work. We find more insights into isolated parts of crisis management than into the larger process. Integration aids practitioners, researchers, and educators. Practitioners gain comprehensive guidelines for managing and preventing crises. Researchers gain a more complete foundation for executing their research. Educators gain an organized set of skills and concepts to teaching future crisis managers. My primary goal with this book is providing an integrative framework for approaching crisis management. My secondary goal is developing new parts of the crisis management process to improve the overall process. Throughout the book, I emphasize the vital role of crisis communication in the crisis management process.

I use a three-staged approach to integrate the various parts and ideas about crisis management into a comprehensive framework. Chapters 1 and 2 provide a detailed explanation of the integration. The first stage is precrisis and involves detecting crises, preventing crises, and preparing for crises. Chapters 3, 4, and 5 examine the precrisis stage. The second stage is the crisis event and involves recognizing the crisis, containing the crisis, and recovering from the crisis. Chapters 6 and 7 cover the crisis event stage. The third and final stage is postcrisis and involves evaluating crisis management efforts, remembering crisis management efforts, and identifying postcrisis actions. Chapter 8 covers the postcrisis stage. Chapter 9 highlights the important lessons offered in the book.

I offer two additional points to guide the reader. First, as suggested by the title, crisis management is taken as an ongoing process. Each stage in the three-staged approach naturally connects to the next, with the postcrisis offering a route back to the precrisis stage. Isolated ideas become integrated into a continuous flow of crisis management and crisis communication. Second, throughout the book are various application points. The application points give the reader an opportunity to apply the concepts being discussed. The reader has a chance to become involved in the material by engaging in the various applications exercises.

Application is a fitting closing point. Crisis management and communication writings must be applied to be of value. An ultimate goal of crisis management research is to improve the practice. Improvement means saving lives, financial resources, and reputations and other valuable resources. I have had the good fortune of fine-tuning many of my ideas with full-time practitioners before trying them myself. Their feedback has strengthened my work. My good fortune is due to the hard work of Larry Barton, now a vice president at Motorola. For the past 7 years, Larry has organized the

New Avenues in Crisis Management Conference. I have been active in the conference for the past 5 years. I end by thanking Larry for facilitating my development as a crisis management researcher, educator, and practitioner.

1

A Need for More Crisis Management Information

People involved in running or reporting about organizations have a healthy appetite for the news. Both practitioners and researchers know that keeping abreast of current events is an aid to their job performance. We all have various ways of accessing the news. We might watch CNN, Fox, MSNBC, or the evening news on television, read newspapers or magazines, listen to NPR or a news station on the radio, or download our news from the many sources on the Internet such as the Associated Press, Reuters, or the Business Wire. We soon learn a valuable lesson from following any news source—crises happen frequently.

No organization is immune to crises. As Marconi (1992) observed, bad things happen to even good organizations. Pick any day of the week and you will find stories about train derailments, plane crashes, funds used inappropriately at a nonprofit organization, explosions in a manufacturing facility, workers shot or injured on the job, or *E. coli*-tainted beef, turkey, chicken, or even bean sprouts. The bottom line—all organizations should learn as much as they can about crisis management.

This book is designed as an aid to those interested in practicing, researching, or teaching crisis management. To those interested in practicing crisis management, the book offers a comprehensive approach for structuring a crisis management program. For those interested in researching crisis management, the book provides an analytical framework for the study of crisis management efforts. Those involved in teaching crisis management are offered an additional resource for educating future crisis managers. The book starts with a definition of crisis, moves to a rationale for the importance of crisis management, and concludes by examining the need for a comprehensive approach to crisis management.

Crisis Management Defined

Although it is very easy to find a book or article about crisis management, it is not so easy to find a standard definition. Having a specific definition is important because how we define a subject indicates how we approach it. Most of the crisis management writings assume we all know or agree with what is meant by crisis management. This book begins by defining *crisis* and then explains what is meant by the concept *crisis management*.

Crisis Defined

What are crisis managers to do if there is no one, accepted definition of a crisis? One option is to survey the existing definitions to develop a foundation for a viable definition. Some sample definitions from seminal crisis management books include the following:

- "turning point for better or worse" (Fink, 1986, p. 15);
- "a major occurrence with a potentially negative outcome affecting an organization, company or industry, as well as its publics, products, services, or good name" (Fearn-Banks, 1996, p. 1);
- "a major unpredictable event that has potentially negative results. The event and its aftermath may significantly damage an organization and its employees, products, services, financial condition, and reputation" (Barton, 1993, p. 2).

We begin to see some common traits emerge from the survey of definitions. These shared traits can be used to form a working definition of a crisis. A crisis can be defined as an event that is an unpredictable, major threat that can have a negative effect on the organization, industry, or stakeholders if handled improperly.

A crisis is unpredictable but not unexpected. Wise organizations know crises will befall them; they just do not know when. Crises strike suddenly, giving them an element of surprise or unpredictability (Barton, 1993; National Research Council, 1996). There are always exceptions to the rule; some crises offer a great deal of warning (Irvine & Millar, 1996). The use of the term *major* means that the organizational routine is disrupted in some way. Pauchant and Mitroff's (1992) differentiation between incidents and crises illustrates the meaning of *major.* An incident is a minor, localized disruption. A water valve breaks and sprays water in the vending and meeting areas of a plant. The valve is repaired, some meetings are rescheduled, and vending machines are down for a day. The valve is replaced without harming the larger organizational routine, making it an incident, not a crisis. If the broken water valve led to the plant being shut down, then it becomes a crisis because it disrupts the entire organization. A crisis does or has the potential to disrupt or affect the entire organization.

Crises are threats, meaning that they actually do or have the potential to create negative or undesirable outcomes. *Threat* is often translated to mean damage. Crisis damage can include financial loss (e.g., lost productivity or a drop in earnings), injuries or deaths to stakeholders, structural or property damage, sullied reputations, and environmental harm (Loewendick, 1993). The crisis threatens a variety of targets. The industry can be affected by a crisis in one of its member organizations. An industry can suffer financial loss (e.g., new, costly regulation) or reputational damage from a crisis as people project the crisis onto an entire industry. The Exxon *Valdez* had such an effect on the petroleum industry. Publics began to worry more about the environmental threat posed by the petroleum industry. Stakeholders can be injured or killed, suffer structural or property damage, or have financial losses. Employees, customers, or community members can be injured or killed by industrial or transportation accidents. A plane crash can kill crew members, customers, and people on the ground. Environmental damage is another outcome of accidents. Community members can suffer structural or property damage from accidents as well. Careless handling of the accident can add to the environmental and structural or property damage. The plane might crash into homes, or a fire from a plant explosion might damage nearby homes. Stockholders can lose money from the costs of the crisis. For example, an organization incurs repair expenses from accidents, and a faulty product can result in product liability lawsuits and recall costs. A crisis presents real or potential negative outcomes for organizations, their stakeholders, and/or their industry. Crisis management is designed to ward off or reduce the threats by providing guidelines for properly handling crises.

Crisis Management

Crisis management represents a set of factors designed to combat crises and lessen the actual damage inflicted by the crisis. Put another way, crisis management seeks to prevent or lessen the negative outcomes of a crisis and thereby protect the organization, stakeholders, and/or industry from damage. There are four basic factors involved in crisis management: prevention, preparation, performance, and learning. Prevention represents steps taken to avoid crises. Crisis managers often detect the warning signs of a crisis and then take actions that prevent the crisis from occurring. For instance, a faulty toaster is recalled before its overheating problem causes any fires or injuries to customers. Prevention goes on unseen by the public. We rarely read news stories about the crisis that did not happen.

Preparation is the best known factor in crisis management because it includes the crisis management plan (CMP). If people know nothing else about crisis management, they know that an organization should have a CMP. The CMP is the tip of the crisis management iceberg. Although people think the CMP is the crisis management process, in actuality most of the crisis management process is unseen. Preparation involves not only the CMP but also diagnosing crisis vulnerabilities, selecting and training the crisis management team and spokespersons, creating the crisis portfolio, and refining the crisis communication system.

Performance is the application of the preparation components to a crisis. The crisis can be simulated or real. The preparation components must be tested regularly. The testing involves running simulated crises and drills that determine the fitness of the CMP, crisis team members, spokespersons, and communication system. A real crisis involves the execution of the same crisis management resources, only the outcomes are real rather than hypothetical. Performance is very public during a real crisis. An organization's crisis management performance is frequently reported and critiqued in the news media (Pearson & Clair, 1998). Many publications dissected Exxon's performance during the *Valdez* oil spill. Remember, crises make for good news stories.

Learning is the fourth crisis factor. During learning the organization evaluates its performance in simulated and real crises. The organization learns by determining what it did right and wrong during its crisis management performance. The organization stores this information for future use. Ideally, the right moves are replayed, and the mistakes are avoided and replaced by more appropriate actions. Learning is the development of an institutional memory. The institutional memory improves the effectiveness of crisis management by expanding the organization's perception of crises and response capacity to crises (Weick, 1988). The more and varied crises an organization experiences through practice sessions, the better it can handle those same crises in reality. The four steps make a complete circle. If prevention fails, preparation is required for optimal performance. Learning is derived from performance and informs both the prevention of and preparation for a crisis. In turn, improving preparation should improve performance. Crisis management is a process of preventing, preparing for, performing, and learning from crises.

Importance of Crisis Management

The first paragraph of this book reminded us that crises are ubiquitous. In fact, today's environment seems to be placing higher premiums on crisis management—unprepared organizations have more to lose today than they ever have before. A variety of environmental developments have made all types of organizations more susceptible to crises (Barton, 1993). In turn, a higher premium is placed on crisis management as mismanagement costs seem to escalate. The new environmental pressures center on stakeholder activism and the news media.

Stakeholder Activism

Today, angry stakeholders are now more likely to generate crises. Stakeholders are becoming increasing more vocal when dealing with organizations (Grunig, 1992; Irvine & Millar, 1996; Mitroff, 1994; Putnam, 1993). Customers have a heightened sense of awareness about consumer issues and are willing to speak out (Maynard, 1993). In 1995, Starbucks faced a negative advertisement in the *Wall Street Journal* placed by a disgruntled customer. The customer was upset because he felt he had been treated poorly when returning two nonfunctioning coffeemakers he had bought as gifts. The story even made the *CBS Evening News*. Disgruntled shareholders have taken control of some corporations ("Chronology," 1994; Star, 1993). Furthermore, activist groups are more organized and prepared to engage in negative publicity campaigns, boycotts, and negative information spread via the Internet (Bradsher, 1996; Mitroff, 1994; Putnam 1993). Moreover, global

companies face conflicting ethical codes, cultural clashes, employee kidnap-
ing, and government intrusion such as nationalization.

New Technology

New communication technologies speed the transmission of communication and help to make the world a smaller place. Crises are now global, thanks
to communication technology. News is global. An event in an isolated area
of Africa appears rapidly around the world. Organizations no longer have
isolated crises because the once remote or far-flung areas of the world are
accessible to the media and to other stakeholders (Birch, 1994; Donath,
1984). The crisis may appear on CNN (or some other international news
service) or be the subject of a Web site on the Internet. Nike's treatment of
workers in the Far East was an international news story, and Greenpeace
documented its battles with Shell Oil over the *Brent Spar* tanker buoy on the
Internet (Adams, 1996; Herbert, 1997). Shell fought back by placing press
releases and research findings on its Web site to justify its decision.

Raising the Stakes

As the potential for crises increases, so do the potential negative outcomes.
The organizations are playing for higher stakes when confronting crises.
Crisis susceptibility escalates the risks of all types of damage, with financial
and reputational damage being most salient (Barton, 1993; Mitroff, 1994).
The end result is a higher premium on effective crisis management. The value
of crisis management is greater now than when experts first began preaching
about the need for crisis preparedness in the late 1970s. Organizations must
continue to improve their crisis management processes. Crisis management
acts as a hedge against the negative outcomes of crises. Effective crisis
management can reduce the time it takes to complete the crisis life cycle,
prevent a loss of sales, limit reputational damage, preclude the development
of public policy issues, save money, and protect lives, health, and the
environment (Barton, 1993; Higbee, 1992).

A Comprehensive Approach

Improving the crisis management process should be easy because so much
has been written about crisis management. Researchers and practitioners

from various branches of management, communication, psychology, and sociology all have contributed their ideas and insights on how to engage in crisis management. The problem is that although vast, the crisis management writings are fragmented (Pearson & Clair, 1998). The multidisciplinary nature of crisis management can obscure the "big picture." Shrivastava (1993) referred to the fragmentation as the "Tower of Babel Effect" (p. 33). Writers often focus on their specialities and fail to make connections to ideas and concepts developed in other specialities. In turn, this fragmentation precludes a fuller understanding of crisis management that is gained by integrating the various perspectives. Practitioners, researchers, and educators are limited by this fractured approach.

Crisis communication strategies illustrate the fragmentation, and they are a subset of crisis communication that focuses on what the organization says and does after a crisis hits. A crisis manager would have to review the business communication, consumer research, rhetoric, organizational communication, and public relations literatures to collect and integrate all the ideas needed to develop guidelines about what to say during a crisis. Such a comprehensive review requires a lot of work for a crisis manager. Researchers and educators are not accomplishing integration to any large degree. Research and reading materials in one discipline often ignore or even duplicate research in another discipline. Ironically, a 1998 article addressing the fragmented nature of crisis management research referenced no communication-based studies (Pearson & Clair, 1998). Virtually all aspects of the crisis management process are plagued by this same fractured approach.

A system that integrates the crisis management writings would benefit practitioners, researchers, and educators. Practitioners will have the lessons and recommendations of crisis management experts synthesized into a usable form. Helpful ideas from a variety of perspectives will be condensed into one consistent framework. The various ideas can be integrated into one comprehensive crisis management process. Researchers will benefit from exposure to fields they may not have known were involved in crisis management. Moreover, the framework will indicate where more research is needed to improve the crisis management process. Educators will have a tool that provides detailed lessons for teaching the crisis management process. The purpose of this book is to provide the needed comprehensive approach to the crisis management process. What follows is a synthesis of the best ideas from the crisis management writings integrated into a comprehensive crisis management process designed to aid managers, researchers, and educators.

2

Outline for an Ongoing Approach to Crisis Management

A good guidebook is a valuable tool whenever you visit a major city for the first time. The guidebook helps you navigate through the unfamiliar streets, restaurants, attractions, and hotels that bombard your senses. People approaching the vast crisis management writings are like the traveler entering a new city. The disparate volumes of crisis management information can be overwhelming. Crisis managers would benefit from a guide to the myriad fragments of crisis management information. A useful guide would provide an overarching framework that allows a crisis manager to integrate the varied pieces of crisis management information into a usable form. This book develops a systematic approach for synthesizing the diverse crisis management insights into one comprehensive framework. Chapter 2 details the development of the comprehensive framework and previews the remaining chapters in the book.

The Initial Crisis Management Framework

The idea that crises have an identifiable life cycle is a consistent theme that permeates the crisis management literature. The crisis manager needs to understand this life cycle because different states in the life cycle require different actions (Gonzalez-Herrero & Pratt, 1995; Sturges, 1994). The crisis life cycle has been translated into what I term *staged approaches* to crisis management. A staged approach means that the crisis management function is divided into discrete segments that are executed in a specific order. Moreover, the life cycle perspective reveals that effective crisis management must be integrated into the normal operations of an organization. Crisis management is not merely developing a plan and executing it during a crisis. Instead, it is appropriately viewed as an ongoing process. Every day, organizational members can be scanning for potential crises and taking actions to prevent them or any number of the aspects of the crisis management process detailed in this book. Crisis management should be a full-time part of many people's jobs in an organization, not a part-time fancy. Each working day, crisis managers can be doing something to improve crisis prevention and response.

The life cycle perspective has yielded a variety of staged approaches to crisis management. The staged approaches provide the mechanism for constructing a framework for organizing the vast and varied crisis management writings. Regardless of the discipline, the various topics addressed in crisis management can be placed within a comprehensive, staged approach to crisis management. A comprehensive framework would organize the scattered crisis management insights and permit crisis mangers to easily envision their best options during any stage of the crisis management process. Crisis managers would benefit by having the wide array of crisis management resources being presented in a more user-friendly format. The current fragmentation of the crisis management literature can leave managers struggling to organize bits of information or even to miss critical resources entirely. A comprehensive set of crisis management insights overcomes the problems of disorganization and omission. Crisis managers will find it easier to access and apply crisis management resources, thereby improving the crisis management process. Developing such a comprehensive framework begins with a review of the staged approaches to crisis management.

Past Staged Approaches
to Crisis Management

Three influential staged approaches emerge from the various crisis management models. Influence was gauged by the number of people citing the approach as an influence in the development of their crisis models. The three most influential staged approaches are Fink's (1986) four-staged model of a crisis life cycle, Mitroff's (1994) five-staged model, and the basic three-staged model. Fink's is the earliest and can be found in his seminal book, *Crisis Management: Planning for the Inevitable.* His crisis life cycle is well represented, even in writings appearing in the 1990s (i.e., Darling, 1994; Sturges, 1994). Fink uses a medical illness metaphor to identify four stages in the crisis life cycle: (a) prodromal—clues or hints that a potential crisis exists begin to emerge; (b) crisis breakout or acute—a triggering event occurs along with the attendant damage; (c) chronic—the effects of the crisis linger as efforts to clean up the crisis progress; and (d) resolution—there is some clear signal that the crisis is no longer a concern to stakeholders; it is over (Fink, 1986).

Fink's (1986) staged approach is one of the first to treat a crisis as an extended event. Of particular note is Fink's belief that warning signs precede the trigger event. The job of crisis managers expands and becomes more proactive when they know and read the warning signs. A well-prepared crisis manager does not just enact the crisis management plan (CMP) when the crisis hits (being reactive), but he or she is also involved in identifying and resolving situations that could become or lead to a crisis (being proactive). In addition, Fink divides the crisis event into three stages. A crisis does not just happen, it evolves. A crisis begins with a trigger event (acute), moves to extended efforts to deal with the crisis (chronic), and concludes with a clear ending (resolution). Different stages of the crisis life cycle require different actions from the crisis manager. As a result, crisis management is enacted in stages and is not one simple action—there is more to crisis management than writing and using the CMP.

Sturges's (1994) elaborations on Fink's (1986) model illustrate how different actions are required during various crisis phases. Sturges argues that different types of communication are emphasized during the various phases of the crisis life cycle. The acute phases are dominated by the eruption of the crisis. Stakeholders do not know what is happening and therefore require information about how the crisis will affect them and what they should do to protect themselves. Information such as whether community members should evacuate an area or whether employees should report for the next shift is highly relevant. In contrast, the resolution stage sees the end of the crisis. Now, stakeholders would be receptive to messages designed to bolster the organization's reputation. Stakeholders need to know how a crisis affects them when it breaks but are open to reputation-building messages once the crisis ends (Sturges, 1994). The demands of the crisis stage dictate what crisis managers can and should be doing at any particular time. The later chapters of this book will detail the different actions required during the various stages of a crisis.

The second influential staged approach is from crisis expert Ian Mitroff (1994). Mitroff divides crisis management into five phases: (a) signal detection—new crisis warning signs should be identified and acted on to prevent a crisis; (b) probing and prevention—organizational members search known crisis risk factors and work to reduce their potential for harm; (c) damage containment—a crisis hits, and organizational members try to prevent the crisis damage from spreading into uncontaminated parts of the organization or its environment; (d) recovery—organizational members work to return to normal business operations as soon as possible; and (e) learning—organizational members review and critique their crisis management efforts, thereby adding to the organization's memory (Mitroff, 1994).

Although subtle differences are apparent, the similarities between the Fink (1986) and Mitroff (1994) staged approaches are strong. Mitroff's stages reflect Fink's crisis life cycle to a large degree. Signal detection and probing can be seen as part of the prodromal phase. The difference is the degree to which the Mitroff model emphasizes detection and prevention. Although Fink's model implies that crises can be prevented, Mitroff's model actively seeks to prevent them.

There is a strong correspondence between the damage containment and crisis breakout stages and the recovery and abatement stages. Both damage containment and crisis breakout focus on the trigger event—a crisis hits. However, Mitroff's (1994) model places greater emphasis on limiting the effects of the crisis. Augustine (1995) and Ammerman (1995) both highlight the need to limit the spread of the crisis to "healthy" parts of the organization. The recovery and chronic stages reflect the natural need to restore normal operations in an organization. In fact, one measure of success for crisis management is the speed with which normal operations are restored (Mitroff, 1994). Mitroff's model emphasizes how the crisis management team can facilitate the recovery, whereas Fink's (1986) model simply documents that organizations can recover at varying speeds.

Both the learning and resolution stages signal the end of the crisis. The additional review and critique of the learning stage are a function of Mitroff's (1994) focus on crisis management rather than just crisis description. Fink's (1986) model simply notes that the resolution stage occurs when a crisis is no longer a concern. For Fink, termination marks the end of the crisis management function. In contrast, Mitroff's model is cyclical because the end also represents the beginning. The crisis management effort is reviewed and critiqued to find ways to improve the crisis management system. The last stage actually signals the start of implementing improvements in the crisis management system. Hence, the learning phase can feed back to either the signal detection phase or the probing and prevention phase. Gonzalez-Herrero and Pratt (1995, 1996) extend Mitroff's thinking by treating the final stage as a continuation of the recovery stage. In addition to evaluation and retooling, the final stage involves maintaining contact with key stakeholders, monitoring the issues tied to the crisis, and providing updates to the media (Gonzalez-Herrero & Pratt, 1995, 1996). Communication and follow-up with stakeholders from the recovery phase are carried over to the learning phase.

The essential difference between the Fink (1986) and Mitroff (1994) phased models is revealed by comparing the last phases of the models. The Mitroff model is active and stresses what crisis managers should do at each phase. The Fink model is more descriptive and stresses the characteristics of each phase. This is not to say that Fink is not offering recommendations to crisis managers. Rather, the Mitroff model is more prescriptive than the Fink model. Fink is concerned with mapping how crises progress, but Mitroff is concerned with how crisis management efforts progress. Early models tend to be descriptive, so this essential difference should not be unexpected.

The three-staged model has no clearly identifiable creator but has been recommended by a variety of crisis management experts (i.e., Birch, 1994; Guth, 1995; Mitchell, 1986; Woodcock, 1994). Crisis management is divided into three macrostages: precrisis, crisis, and postcrisis. *Macro* means that the stages are more general and that each stage contains a number of more specific substages, the microlevel. This is similar to economics, where macroeconomics deals with all the forces at work on the economy, and microeconomics deals with the specific factors affecting the economy. Both the Fink (1986) and Mitroff (1994) models fit naturally within the three-stage approach. The precrisis stage encompasses all aspects of crisis preparation. Prodromal/signal detection and probing would be included in the precrisis stage. The crisis stage includes the actions taken to cope with the crisis or trigger event—the time span when the crisis is being resolved. Damage containment/crisis breakout and recovery/chronic all fall within the crisis stage. The postcrisis stage reflects the period after the crisis is considered to be over or resolved. Learning and resolution are each a part of the postcrisis stage. Crisis management experts from diverse fields agree that crises do have life cycles and that these life cycles affect the crisis management process. The life cycles concept underlies the three similar staged approaches to crisis management. A staged approach offers a mechanism for integrating the diverse crisis management writings and creating a unified set of crisis management guidelines.

Outline of the
Three-Staged Approach

The three-staged approach to crisis management was selected as the organizing framework for this book because of its ability to subsume the other staged approaches used in crisis management. The ideal crisis management model could accommodate all of the various models plus additional insights provided by other crisis management experts. Not all crisis managers placed their ideas within a phased model. Therefore, a comprehensive model must be able to place "random" insights into the crisis management process. The three-staged approach to crisis management has the appropriate macrolevel generality for constructing the comprehensive framework necessary for analyzing the crisis management literature. The three stages are general enough to accommodate the other two dominant crisis management models and to allow for the integration of ideas from other crisis management experts. Within each stage, separate substages or sets of actions that should be covered during that stage.

The three-staged approach provides the organizing framework for the book. Each substage integrates a cluster of writings about that particular crisis management topic. Each cluster of writings was carefully examined to distill the essential recommendations the clusters could offer to crisis managers. For each substage, the crisis wisdom and any tests of that wisdom are reported along with a discussion of its utility to crisis managers. Moreover, the staged approach provides a unified system for organizing and using the varied insights crisis managers offer. The progression of the book follows the three-staged approach.

Precrisis

Chapters 3, 4, and 5 are devoted to the development of the precrisis stage. Organizational members should be proactive and take all possible actions to prevent crises. The precrisis stage entails actions that organizational members should perform before a crisis is encountered. However, not all crises can be prevented, so organizational members must prepare for crises as well. The precrisis stage involves three substages: signal detection, prevention, and crisis preparation.

Chapter 3 deals with signal detection. Most crises do emit early warning signs. If early action is taken, these crises can be avoided (Gonzalez-Herrero & Pratt, 1995). Crisis managers must identify sources for warning signs, collect information related to warning signs, and analyze the information for warning signs. For example, a pattern in customer complaints could identity a product defect. Reporting the complaints to the appropriate manufacturing sector of the organization can result in corrective action being taken. In turn, the corrective action prevents further complaints and the potential of a highly visible recall and/or battle with customers. Crisis managers must develop a system for detecting potential crises and responding to them.

Chapter 3 also marks the introduction of the application points. The application points provide the reader with an opportunity to apply concepts and ideas being discussed in the book. Each application point is presented as an individual exercise. The lessons can be extended by exchanging your answers with another person. Understanding additional perspectives on each exercise expands what you can learn from the application points.

Chapter 4 is devoted to crisis prevention. Once detected, actions must be taken to prevent the crisis. Preventative measures fall into three categories: issues management, risk aversion, and relationship building. Issues management takes steps to prevent an issue from maturing into a crisis. Risk aversion eliminates or lowers risk levels. Relationship building means that various organizational units, primarily those involved in the public relations functions, work to cultivate positive relationships with the organization's key stakeholders. The cornerstone of the positive relationship is open communication between members of the organization and the stakeholders. A dialogue develops as the organization and stakeholders exchange opinions, information, and even tangible resources en route to identifying and resolving any potential problems in the relationship (Grunig, 1992). Chapter 5 develops the idea of crisis preparation. Crisis managers must be prepared for when a crisis does happen. Preparation typically involves identifying crisis vulnerabilities, creating crisis teams, selecting spokespersons, drafting CMPs, developing crisis portfolios (a list of the most likely crises to befall an organization), and structuring the crisis communication system.

Crisis Event

The crisis event stage begins with a trigger event that marks the beginning of the crisis. The crisis stage ends when the crisis is considered to be resolved. During the crisis event, crisis managers must realize that the organization is in crisis and take appropriate actions. Communication with stakeholders is a critical facet of this phase. An organization communicates to stakeholders through its words and actions. The crisis phase has three substages: crisis recognition, crisis containment, and business resumption.

Chapter 6 is devoted to crisis recognition. People in an organization must realize that a crisis exists and respond to the event as a crisis. Crisis recognition includes an understanding of how events get labeled and accepted as crises—how to sell a crisis to management—and the means for collecting crisis-related information. Chapter 7 covers both crisis containment and business resumption. Crisis containment focuses on the organization's crisis response, including the importance and content of how the initial response is explained, communication's relationship to reputational management, contingency plans, and follow-up concerns.

Postcrisis

Organizations must consider what to do when a crisis is deemed to be "over." Postcrisis actions help to (a) make the organization better prepared for the next crisis, (b) make sure stakeholders are left with a positive impression of the organization's crisis management efforts, and (c) check to make sure that the crisis is truly over. Chapter 8 addresses evaluating crisis management, learning from the crisis, and continuing postcrisis actions such as follow-up communication with stakeholders and continued monitoring of issues related to the crisis.

Summary

The book ends with a summary of key ideas. The final chapter highlights some of the major contributions this book can offer to practitioners, researchers, and educators.

3

Signal Detection

The best way to manage a crisis is to prevent it. Although all crises cannot be prevented, many can be (Pauchant & Mitroff, 1992). Crises are avoided by recognizing the warning signs, what Fink (1986) calls prodromes. The warning signs or prodromes indicate that a situation has the potential to develop into a crisis. The effective crisis manager detects these prodromes and takes action to defuse the situation. If all goes as planned, the crisis manager has averted a crisis. Crisis management must include mechanisms designed to scan and monitor for crisis warning signals. This chapter explores the elements involved in signal detection.

The basic element of signal detection is scanning, an active search for information. Crisis managers must scan for information that might contain prodromes. A variety of information sources must be scanned due to the diversity of crises that could befall an organization. The crisis managers must scan the environment and internal events for warning signs. Part of scanning is the analysis of information. The crisis managers must evaluate the information they have collected for prodromes. Those prodromes with the greatest potential are then monitored for further developments. Scanning is a form of radar; it identifies as many prodromes as possible. Monitoring is a form of focused tracking, and it keeps a close watch on the prodromes that have the greatest potential to become crises. Therefore, the signal detection stage must be able to collect and analyze information that may contain prodromes.

Signal detection is a tri-part process. First, the sources of information to be scanned must be identified. The crisis managers want to search sources that are related to crises in some way. For instance, customer complaints can signal a potential crisis in product quality or customer relations. Second, the information must be collected. The crisis managers must decide how the information will be collected from the source. And third, the information must be evaluated for its crisis potential. Crisis managers must evaluate how strong the prodrome is—how likely the situation is to develop into a crisis. Scanning is a systematic search and analysis of events. Crisis managers scan both outside of the organization (the environment) and inside of the organization for warning signs. Neglecting either area could result in crisis managers overlooking important warning signs of an impeding crisis.

Contributing Organizational Functions

So how does a crisis manager go about building a scanning system? The first step is to examine existing scanning resources. Issues management, risk assessment, and stakeholder relations all serve to scan information that could be relevant to crisis management. Examining the three functions provides the materials necessary to construct a crisis-sensing mechanism.

Issues Management

An issue is "a trend or condition . . . that, if continued, would have a significant effect on how a company is operated" (Moore, 1979, p. 43). An issue is a type of problem whose resolution can affect the organization. Issues management tries to lessen the negative impact of an issue. Issues management is a systematic approach intended to shape how the issue develops and is resolved. It is a proactive attempt to have an issue decided in a way favorable to an organization. Although issues management can address internal concerns (Dutton & Jackson, 1987; Dutton & Ottensmeyer, 1987), the emphasis is on societal and political issues that populate the organization's environment—external issues (Coombs, 1992). Societal issues relate to standards of corporate social performance (Heath & Cousino, 1990), whereas potential political issues involve regulatory and legislative decisions (Buchholz, 1990; Hainsworth, 1990). Issues management includes the identification of and actions taken to affect issues (Heath, 1990). Because some issues can develop into crises, issues management contributes to crisis scanning (Gonzalez-Herrero & Pratt, 1996).

Risk Assessment

Risk assessment attempts to identify risk factors or weaknesses and to assess the probability that a weakness will be exploited or developed into crises (Levitt, 1997; Pauchant & Mitroff, 1992). Every organization faces a variety of risk factors. Typical risk factors include personnel, products, the production process, facilities, competition, regulations, and customers (Barton, 1993). The risk factors exist as a normal part of an organization's operation. The following incidents illustrate the crisis potential of risk factors. In March 1996, a Marine at Camp Pendleton shot and killed his lieutenant, then shot another superior officer—employee risk. In December 1996, a blast at the Wyman Gordon Forging Company metal-fabricating plant near Houston, Texas, blew a hole in the roof, killing eight workers and injuring two others—production process risk. Although not daily events, the existence of employees, production processes, and other risk factors can lead to serious crises, and no organization is immune. Risk can never be eliminated completely. Risk assessment has more of an internal rather than an external focus. The internal weaknesses identified through risk assessment provide vital information for crisis management scanning. For instance, Occupational Safety and Health Administration records might reveal a pattern of mishandling acid spills. The crisis team would look for ways to break the pattern, thereby preventing injuries and reducing a crisis-inducing risk factor.

Stakeholder Relationships

Crisis experts agree that favorable organization-stakeholder relationships are a benefit during crisis management (e.g., Fearn-Banks, 1996; Slahor, 1989). But what does the term *relationship* mean? Talking about organizational relationships with stakeholders assumes that we all understand and agree on what is meant by relationship and stakeholder. For crisis management, a useful definition of relationship is the interdependence of two or more people or groups. This definition is a modification of one developed by O'Hair, Friedrich, Wiemann, and Wiemann (1995). The definition centers on interdependence, some factor that binds the two people or groups together. The interdependence definition of relationship is useful because it is consistent with the stakeholder theory that guides most business thinking (Rowley, 1997).

Stakeholder theory posits that an organization's environment is populated with various stakeholders. An organization survives or thrives by effectively managing these stakeholders (Clarkson, 1991; Wood, 1991). Stakeholders are generally defined as any person or group that has an interest, right, claim, or ownership in an organization. Stakeholders have been separated into two distinct groups: primary and secondary. Primary stakeholders are those people or groups whose actions can be harmful or beneficial to an organization. Failure to maintain a continuing interaction with a primary stakeholder could result in the failure of the organization. Typical primary stakeholders include employees, investors, customers, suppliers, and the government. For instance, organizations cannot operate without employees, and government officials may close a facility for a variety of legal or regulatory reasons. Secondary stakeholders or influencers are those people or groups who can affect or be affected by the actions of an organization. Typical influencers include the media, activist groups, and competitors. Influencers cannot stop an organization from functioning but still can damage an organization (Clarkson, 1995; Donald & Preston, 1995).

Primary and secondary stakeholders are interdependent with an organization, thus the relevance of the earlier definition of relationship. Each of the stakeholders and the organization have a connection that links them in some way. The links include economic, social, and political concerns. In reality, the concept of stakeholder management is the management of the relationship between the organization and its various stakeholders. Organizational success is predicated on maintaining an effective balance in these relationships (Donaldson & Preston, 1995; Rowley, 1997; Savage, Nix, Whitehead, & Blair, 1991). Most public relations theorists agree with this assessment (e.g., Grunig, 1992). It follows that stakeholders can play an important role in crisis management.

Primary stakeholders can stop organizational operations and trigger a crisis. Conflict with an organization can lead primary stakeholders to withhold their contributions. As a result, an organization will stop operating if those contributions cannot be replaced. For instance, unhappy workers can strike, and discontented customers can boycott. In 1997, the Teamsters' 15-day strike against UPS cost the company $600 million in revenues. A total of 185,000 Teamsters, nearly two thirds of the UPS American workforce, joined the strike. At its best, UPS was able to operate at only 10% capacity using management personnel and drivers who did not strike. UPS found it could not function without the contributions of the drivers, so UPS conceded to their demands (Sewell, 1997).

In 1996, PepsiCo announced that it would begin to sever all ties with Myanmar (formerly Burma). PepsiCo acknowledged consumer pressure as the primary reason for its decision. Since 1993, PepsiCo had been a boycott target because its facilities in Myanmar helped to support that country's human rights-abusing government. Major customers—cities and universities—began to deny PespiCo their business (contributions) (Cooper, 1997; Freeman, 1996). Primary stakeholders are powerful because it is difficult and often impossible to replace the contributions that they provide the organization (Mitchell, Agle, & Wood, 1997).

For crisis management, it would be a mistake to focus solely on primary stakeholders. Problems in relationships with secondary stakeholders can also trigger crises. The media can expose organizational misdeeds or generate other negative publicity, competitors can instigate lawsuits that bind an organization's operations, and activists can launch boycotts or protests against an organization. A few examples will illustrate the role of secondary stakeholders in creating crises.

On November 7, 1997, the investigative news show *Dateline* aired a story about Sears. The story documented how some Sears stores were reselling returned or damaged batteries as new. The president of the Sears Automotive Division denied all charges at first. The evidence against Sears included three batteries *Dateline* had tested and the testimony of former employees. A Sears manufacturing executive said that the laboratory tests were bad science with improper interpretations of the corrosion data and that the former employees were not credible because they lacked documentation. Then, *Dateline* secretly marked and returned two batteries to different stores in the Washington, D.C. area. One of the batteries was returned to the shelves as a "new" battery. The president of the Sears Automotive Division requested another interview. This time, Sears admitted to problems, announced an internal investigation to solve the battery problem, and thanked *Dateline* for bringing this problem to their attention. A media representative had precipitated a crisis.

In June 1996, Boehringer Mannheim, a German-owned drug and medical device company, sued Johnson & Johnson's diabetes products subsidiary LifeScan for industrial espionage. The charges included stealing a prototype diabetes monitoring system and infiltrating private meetings at Boehringer. Mannheim claimed that LifeScan employees received awards for spying. The awards were named for famous detectives, including the "Inspector Clouseau Award" and the "Columbo Award." The awards were said to include prizes too. The case was based on the testimony of a former LifeScan employee.

LifeScan admitted to some improper activities but claimed they derived no competitive advantages from the information. A competitor had used a lawsuit to embarrass an organization and injure its reputation.

In both cases, a secondary stakeholder had influenced organizational actions. Secondary, as well as primary, stakeholders can create a crisis for an organization. I use the term *key stakeholder* to indicate any group that can precipitate a crisis. As Grunig (1992) notes, mismanaging a stakeholder relationship can produce a crisis. Therefore, watching the organization-stakeholder relationships contributes to crisis scanning.

Summary

Issues management, risk assessment, and stakeholder relations all can contribute to crisis scanning. Combined, the three functions provide a broad-reaching radar system for detecting prodromes. The challenge for crisis managers is to integrate the three organizational functions into an effective crisis-sensing mechanism. To meet the challenge, crisis managers should know what sources to scan, how to collect information, and how to evaluate information for its crisis potential. The next three sections help us to understand the basic elements needed to construct a crisis-sensing mechanism.

Sources to Be Scanned

Crisis managers cannot begin looking for prodromes until they know what sources they will be scanning. Issues management, risk assessment, and stakeholder relations involve a variety of organizational units in the collection of information that should be of interest to crisis managers. Table 3.1 provides a list of the potential crisis sources derived from the information sources of these three functions. The information sources are divided into issues management sources (external information), risk assessment sources, and relationships. The explanation of the potential crisis sources will follow this functional division.

Issues Management Sources

Environmental scanning is a tool that is popular in issues management (Gonzalez-Herrero & Pratt, 1996; Heath, 1997; Heath & Nelson, 1986; Pauchant & Mitroff, 1992). Roughly, environmental scanning watches the

TABLE 3.1 Potential Crisis Sources to Monitor

Issues management sources
    Traditional
        News media

Newspapers	Television news
News and business magazines	
Trade journals	Medical and science journals
Newsletters	Government publications
Public opinion polls	Public opinion experts
Stakeholders	

    Online
        News and business wires
        Online newspapers, magazines, and trade publications
        Archives for professional associations, special interest groups, and government agencies

Newsgroups	Web pages

Risk assessment sources

Total quality management	Liability exposure	Natural disaster exposure
Environmental crisis exposure	Criminal exposure	Product tampering exposure
Legal compliance audits	Financial audits	Ethical climate surveys
Workers compensation exposure	Safety/accident records	Behavioral profiling

Relationship sources
    Shareholder resolutions   Corporate social performance
    Stakeholder complaints/inquiries, including public criticism

environment for changes, trends, events, and emerging social, political, or health issues. The information is used to guide organizational decision making—to plot future actions (Lauzen, 1995). Unfortunately, environmental scanning strategies used by organizations are not well developed (Dyer, 1996). Still, crisis managers must consider the sources involved in external scanning that would be helpful in locating prodromes.

External scanning uses traditional and online sources. The traditional information sources will be discussed followed by the online sources. A common, traditional source used to monitor the environment is to watch, listen to, or read the news media (Heath, 1988). The news media include leading or elite newspapers (e.g., *New York Times, Wall Street Journal,* and the *Washington Post*), news and business magazines (e.g., *Time, Newsweek, Fortune,* etc.), and television news programs such as the evening news and TV news magazines (e.g., *60 Minutes* and *20/20*). Futurists such as John Naisbitt locate trends and issues by examining the media (Heath, 1997). Of special interest are stories about crises in similar organizations. Case studies of similar organizations in crisis are a valuable resource for crisis managers. Similar cases allow the crisis team to learn from someone else's crisis rather than their own (Pauchant & Mitroff, 1992).

Other useful publications include trade journals and information, relevant medical or science journals, newsletters, and public opinion surveys. The trade outlets are likely to carry stories about crises suffered by similar organizations. The trade journals and other publications provide information about issues the industry is facing as well as industry-specific complaints. Both industry-specific issues and complaints may help to identify possible crises for an individual organization within that industry. Medical or science journals may contain studies that might affect how people view your industry. The dangers of cholesterol and concerns over car phones and accident rates are two such examples. The public's first exposure to these two health concerns were through the medical and science publications, not the news media.

Newsletters include reports published by special interest groups, foundations, and government agencies. Each can indicate potential threats to an organization. Special interest publications inform organizations about the concerns of the activist stakeholders and indicate if their anger is being focused on their industry or their specific organization. Foundations can identify emerging issues for the organization. The government publications offer insights into possible regulatory or legal changes as well as identifying emerging issues. For example, the *Federal Register* has information about potential regulatory changes, the *Congressional Record* and *Congressional Quarterly Weekly Report* provide information about new legislation, and the *Congressional Quarterly Researcher* provides information about salient issues in U.S. society. Public opinion surveys can indicate changes in attitudes, lifestyles, or values (Heath, 1997).

People are another source of environmental information. Crisis managers should focus on two broad categories: the public opinion experts and their own stakeholders. Public opinion experts, like the published data, provide insights into public attitudes, lifestyles, or values. Stakeholders can tell the organization how they feel about issues and organizational actions (Heath & Nelson, 1986). It is easy to become overly dependent on the mass media and forget about people as resources for environmental information.

Online resources are becoming more popular in environmental scanning (Heath, 1997; Thomsen, 1995). A crisis team can find online news and business wire services, newspapers, magazines, trade journals, archives from professional associations, special interest groups, and government bodies. The array is similar to the published sources but stored and accessed electronically. This information may have a searchable archive or offer live, continuous feeds of information. Another option is to hire a service that will search for stories on specific topics or provide industry-specific news and information. The online options simply provide information more quickly and make it easier to track events over time (Thomsen, 1995).

Information spreads through the Internet by ways other than the conventional media or publication sources. Newsgroups and Web pages are two information sources that should not be overlooked. Newsgroups are areas where people post and respond to statements about a particular topic (Bobbitt, 1995). A person e-mails in a message to a newsgroup that other people can then read and write responses to if they choose to do so. The continued discussion of a topic is called a thread. There are thousands of newsgroups on any topic imaginable (Gagnon, 1994). Organizations should locate and monitor newsgroups that are related to the organization. For instance, a pharmaceutical company might monitor reactions to the company or discussions of issues related to its product lines in health and wellness newsgroups. Newsgroups can also be monitored for complaints, criticisms, and rumors. A newsgroup is another way of "listening" to what stakeholders are saying about your organization or issues related to your organization (Coombs, 1996).

Web sites are a form of cyberspace library. People can visit and collect information from the Web site. The home page is a table of contents/opening screen for a Web site. The table of contents lists whatever information the Web coordinator (the operator of the Web page) chooses to place at the Web site. A Web site is typically a mix of original information and links to related information. Each Web site has a unique address. By entering the address into a Web navigator, a person is taken to the Web site. Another option is to use a hypertext link. A Web site may contain hypertext links—text in a different color that, when clicked, will take a person to a new Web site (Bobbit, 1995; Wolpin, 1995). It does not matter how people arrive at Web sites; what matters to organizations is what some Web sites contain. Disgruntled stakeholders can voice complaints, criticisms, and spread rumors through a Web page. If you were to type in http://www.saigon.com while on the Web, you would arrive at the Nike Boycott Page. This anti-Nike Web site details Nike's continuing problems with mistreating workers in its Southeast Asia facilities. The Web site contains fact sheets on Nike's Asian labor, a variety of reports, and a media archive, including a 10-page transcript of the

48 Hours broadcast on October 17, 1996, which served to bring the Nike labor problem to the attention of the American people. Web sites may also supply information about issues relevant to an organization. An organization concerned with human rights, for example, can peruse a variety of human rights-oriented Web sites to get a feel for stakeholder sentiments and the development of human rights issues.

The Internet is a source that organizations should not overlook. Scanning involves collecting information from as many sources as possible. Although the Internet user population is still rather small, it does represent an important environmental information resource (Thomsen, 1995). The Internet can be used to access information also found in print or broadcast form, or the Internet can be used to collect information unique to newsgroups and Web pages.

Risk Assessment Sources

The risk assessment sources provide information about the organization's weaknesses that could become crises. This section briefly explains each source and notes its connection to certain crises. Total quality management systematically assesses the manufacturing process to improve quality. Part of that process is to locate sources of defects (Milas, 1996). Product defects can trigger recall crises (Mitroff, 1994). Environmental crisis exposure includes pollution abatement actions and threats to the environment posed by the organization. Polluting can lead to accidents, lawsuits, protests, or regulatory fines. Legal compliance audits make sure the organization is complying with all federal, state, and local laws and regulations. Failure to comply can result in lawsuits or fines. Financial audits review the financial health of the organization. The financial health can indicate financially oriented crises such as hostile takeovers or shareholder rebellion.

Traditional insurance coverage indicates risks worth insuring against. Insurance risks include liability exposure, criminal exposure, and workers compensation exposure. All three areas can produce lawsuits and extremely negative publicity. Natural disaster exposure identifies what mother nature might do to the organization. The organization must know if facilities are at risk of crises driven by floods, earthquakes, or volcanoes—natural actions typically are not covered by insurance. Safety, maintenance, and accident records reveal minor problems that could become crises. These records should be examined for patterns. A series of minor problems run the risk of escalating into major crises. If there are a number of small hand injuries with a piece of equipment, it is possible that a major injury such as amputation or death could also occur. Action should be taken in the prevention phase to break the pattern of minor accidents. Similarly, a history of the same safety violation indicates that a major accident or injury could occur. Safety precautions are designed to prevent accidents and injuries. Unheeded, the workplace becomes unsafe and ripe for accidents and injuries (Komaki, Heinzmann, & Lawson, 1980).

Product tampering exposure examines the manufacturing process and packaging for susceptibility to product tampering. Product tampering leads to recalls and lawsuits. Behavioral profiling identifies the characteristics of potentially dangerous employees, typically those who may become violent. Violent employees can trigger workplace violence crises. Ethical climate surveys assess the organization for temptations and cultural blinders to problems. The blinders are located by examining management attitudes and values about important concerns such as sexual harassment. A weak ethical climate can encourage organizational misdeeds such as check fraud, sexual harassment, or racial discrimination (Mitroff & McWinney, 1987; Soper, 1995).

Astra USA, a subsidiary of Swedish drug giant Astra, illustrates the danger of a weak ethical climate. The May 13, 1996, issue of *Business Week* had the words "Abuse of Power" over a drawing of a man drinking and making inappropriate advances toward a woman. The headline below the picture indicated that an "astonishing" story of sexual harassment at Astra USA could be found inside the magazine. The nine-page story was the result of an investigation that included interviews with more than 70 former and current Astra USA employees. The initial training and national sales meetings were the centerpieces for sexual harassment. During initial training, senior managers often called female trainees down to the bar for late-night drinking and dancing, which frequently ended in the managers' rooms. Trainees feared that offending the male managers would hurt their careers. One woman, a former sales rep, indicated that women had to visit the bar. Managers used their power and authority to suggest that a rep could lose her job if she did not go (Maremont, 1996). Those female reps who played along the best became part of "The Chosen." They were regularly brought back to headquarters for senior management dinners and other corporate functions. Another female rep remembers a drunken top manager grabbing her at a national sales meeting and shouting that she was his and for others to stay away

(Maremont, 1996). The initial training and national sales meetings were an opportunity for the top male managers to use their power over female reps—to engage in sexual harassment.

The recurring theme was that CEO Lars Bildman had fostered an environment of harassment—managers were expected to treat women as sex objects, and women were supposed to accept management's advances if they wanted to rise in the company. The investigation noted that sexual harassment had become a part of the corporate culture at Astra USA. Lars Bildman was forced to resign as a result of the investigation (Maremont, 1996). Astra paid $9.58 million in fines to the Equal Employment Opportunity Commission after admitting women employees were asked for sexual favors in return for favorable treatment on the job ("Harassment," 1998). Astra USA's weak ethical culture led to a crisis that became front-page news. The same fate can befall any company that fails to monitor and correct its own ethical climate.

Relationship Sources

Unlike issues management and risk assessment, the sources for relationship monitoring are not well developed, but Table 3.1 identifies some logical choices. Shareholder resolutions reflect the values and attitudes of those owning stocks. Resolutions can reflect social concerns, such as divestment in South Africa, or financial concerns, such as resolutions preventing the "poison pill" as a takeover defense. The shareholder resolutions provide insight into how the stockholders feel about important issues or the organization itself. Stakeholder complaints or inquires help to detect discontent among customers and discover rumors. Early identification of discontent means the organization can act to resolve the problem and make the customer happy—maintain a positive relationship with this stakeholder (Dozier, 1992). Nike could have avoided an embarrassing and costly mistake by taking stakeholder complaints more seriously.

On June 24, 1997, Nike recalled 38,000 pairs of athletic shoes and apologized to Muslims. Nike had offended Muslims with a flame logo on a basketball shoe that resembled the Arabic script for "Allah." In September 1996, a Muslim distributor in the Middle East raised the first concerns about the design and recommended some modifications to make the logo acceptable to Muslims. Nike made some minor changes of its own. In March 1997, the Council on American Islamic Relations informed Nike that the "new" logo it saw on the basketball shoes looked like the Arabic script for "Allah" and that it was offensive to Muslims. The second complaint resulted in a recall and an apology by Nike ("Muslim Concerns," 1997). Had Nike officials taken the original complaint more seriously, there would have been no recall, and Nike would not have offended an important segment of its customers.

One form of complaint is public criticisms of the organization. Heath (1988) recommends that "all public criticism should prompt corporate leaders and operations managers to conduct studies to determine whether the charges are true and whether key publics are believing the allegations" (p. 105). Inquiries may reveal a rumor as people call to confirm the information they heard in a rumor. The mythic Procter & Gamble (P & G) devil case illustrates the importance of rumor inquiries. Throughout the 1980s and 1990s, P & G has fought a rumor linking it to the devil. Supposedly, a P & G spokesperson had appeared on a television talk show. During the show, the spokesperson said the founder of P & G had sold his soul to the devil for success in business and that P & G still pledges profits to the Church of Satan. The rumor was fueled by pamphlets of the story being given out in schools and churches. P & G ignored the original devil inquiries, thinking they were silly. However, by 1982, P & G was logging 15,000 devil-related calls a month. Truth packets, with testimonials from major religious figures in the United States, were created and distributed. The devil rumors linger to this day. Procter & Gamble ignored the early warning signs about the devil worshiping rumors, a move it regretted later (Newsom, Turk, & Kruckeberg, 1996; Wilcox, Ault, & Agee, 1995).

Corporate social performance reflects how stakeholders feel about the organization's efforts to be socially responsible. Corporate social performance can be measured by examining community relations, treatment of women and minorities, employee relations, treatment of the environment, and quality of services and products (Turban & Greening, 1997). Weaknesses in any one of these areas could develop into a conflict with certain stakeholders. For instance, neglect of community relations can lead to protests from community groups or new local regulations that will hurt the organization in some fashion. The organization-stakeholder relationship evaluation is a direct measure of how stakeholders feel about an organization. Chapter 4 will extend the discussion of social performance and how it informs the evaluation of organization-stakeholder relationships. Again, the organization-stakeholder relationship evaluation locates problems that, if unaddressed, can become crises. Unhappy stakeholders might take their problem public by using protests, boycotts, lawsuits, or other forms of confrontation.

Information Collection

Once potential environmental information sources are located, crisis managers face the challenge of gathering the information from these sources. Content analysis, interviews, surveys, focus groups, and informal contacts are among the most frequently used collection tools. A familiarity with these information collection tools is an important crisis management asset. This section reviews how crisis managers might use the information collection tools.

The earlier statement about watching, reading, or listening to the mass media was an overly simplistic representation of scanning. When using any published, online, or broadcast source, content analysis can be useful. Content analysis involves the systematic coding and classification of written materials. The written materials may be news stories, other publications, or transcripts of focus groups or interviews (Baskin & Aronoff, 1988). To be systematic requires the development of coding categories and training people to use the categories. Coding categories are "the boxes" in which the crisis team places information. Each category has a thorough written definition that indicates what is appropriate for the category. These categories must be mutually exclusive—no message should fit into more than one category (Berelson, 1952). People who will use the categories, the coders, must be trained in their use. Coders must be able to place the same messages in the same categories. This consistency is called reliability. Reliability allows different people to code different messages but still be consistent in the application of the categories. Such consistency allows for comparisons of the coded data. Content analysis converts the written information into quantifiable data—the words become numbers that can be analyzed using statistics (Newsom et al., 1996). Some examples will help to clarify the content analysis process.

Most organizations have established categories for accidents and safety violations. People are trained to understand the differences in the accident and safety categories so that they can accurately record these events. An organization can examine the data to see if certain accidents or safety violations have increased or decreased over time. For example, an organization might be interested in the number of falls in a particular area of the organization. Systematic coding of accidents permits an accurate analysis of the fall data. Similarly, organizations should develop categories for coding customer complaints. It is not enough to know the shear number of complaints sent; an airline, for example, needs to know the type and frequency of different varieties of complaints. By categorizing customer complaints, organizations can identify problem areas by the growth of complaints in that area. If an airline receives increasing complaints about how canceled flights are handled, the airline needs to improve its customer service relative to canceled flights. Systematic coding allows for comparisons that could not be made if the written information had not been quantified. It is the recording of the material that qualifies content analysis as a form of information collecting.

Interviews, surveys, focus groups, or key contacts can be used to collect information from stakeholders. Actually, the first step in soliciting information from stakeholders is for the crisis team to construct a stakeholder map that lists all possible organizational stakeholders (Grunig & Repper, 1992). Then the crisis team would identify the stakeholders relevant to the highest-ranked crises. Interviewers ask people questions about the subject in an organized fashion. The interviewer develops and follows an interview schedule. Preparation is essential. The person collecting the information must have an organized approach to the interview if it is to yield useful information (Stewart & Cash, 1997). Surveys collect information about people's perceptions, attitudes, and opinions. Surveys can be conducted by having people complete questionnaires or by having researchers ask stakeholders the questions from the survey. Focus groups are a collection of specific stakeholders who are brought together to listen and respond to questions as a group. Open-ended questions are used to encourage interaction and to probe the nature of people's beliefs. Key contacts are community, industry, or organizational leaders who are selected because of their expertise on a subject. Using public opinion or issue experts is a form of key contact (Baskin & Aronoff, 1988).

Information Analysis

Collecting information about issues, risks, and stakeholder relationships is of no value unless it is analyzed to determine if the information contains prodromes. Crisis managers determine if the information really does suggest that a crisis is possible. The premise behind finding warning signs early is to locate those that can significantly affect the organization and to take action to manage them (Dutton & Duncan, 1987; Gonzalez-Herrero & Pratt, 1996; Heath & Nelson, 1986). Analysis is the process of understanding if and how a warning sign might affect the organization (Heath & Nelson, 1986). Crisis

managers need criteria for evaluating issues, risks, and stakeholder relationships. This section outlines how crisis managers can evaluate information
about issues, risks, and stakeholder relations.

Issues Evaluation

Two criteria stand out for evaluating issues: likelihood and impact (Heath,
1988, 1997). Likelihood is the probability of an issue gaining momentum.
An issue with momentum is developing and more likely to affect the organization. Some indicators of momentum are sophisticated promotion of the
issue, heavy mass media coverage, and/or a strong self-interest link between
the issue and stakeholders. The anti-Alar campaign illustrates an issue with
momentum. Alar is a chemical that was used to treat apples. Within a year
of launching its campaign, the anti-Alar coalition headed by the Natural
Resources Defense Council (NRDC) had removed Alar from use. The Alar
issue had professionals crafting the publicity effort—sophisticated promotion. Celebrity appearances, including Meryl Streep, helped to garner massive publicity and heavy media coverage. In addition, Alar was treated as a
threat to innocent children, a strong self-interest link between Alar and
consumers (Center & Jackson, 1995).

Impact is how strongly the issue can affect either profits or operations.
Impact involves the use of forecasting, which projects the potential effect of
the issue on the organization. At least 150 forecasting techniques are used in
business. A detailed discussion of forecasting is beyond the scope of this
book. Organizations should use those forecasting methods with which they
are familiar. Ewing (1979), Heath (1997), and Coates, Coates, Jarratt, and
Heinz (1986) offer more details on forecasting techniques. Only issues with
high impact would be considered crises because a crisis must be disruptive
to organizational operations.

Issues can be given a score from 1 to 10 for the two dimensions of
likelihood and impact. The highest-scoring issues should be tracked further,
and the organization should consider taking action to prevent or lessen the
threat of the issue.

Risk Evaluation

Not all risks have the potential to be crises. Crisis managers must be able
to separate the minor risks from the crisis-producing risks. Two criteria can
be used to evaluate risk: likelihood and impact. Likelihood is the probability

that the risk can or will become an event—the risk will cause something to happen. This determines the possibility of the risk being exploited or maturing into an event. Impact is how much the event might affect the organization. Impact includes disruption to organizational routines and potential damage to people, facilities, processes, or reputation (Levitt, 1997). Again, the impact must be strong enough to warrant labeling the event as a crisis. Each risk should be rated on a 1 to 10 scale for both likelihood and impact. The scores high enough to be deemed crises should be identified for preventative action. Although an organization might want to manage all risks (Smallwood, 1995), time and resource constraints will allow organizations to address only the top-priority risks (Heath, 1997).

Stakeholder Evaluation

Stakeholder relationships can experience problems. If stakeholders have concerns, they can become a threat to an organization by taking action against the organization. Not all stakeholder threats are crises. Crisis managers must be able to differentiate between mild and crisis stakeholder threats. Three criteria can be used to evaluate the crisis potential of stakeholder threats: power, legitimacy, and willingness (Mitchell et al., 1997). Power is the ability of the stakeholder to get the organization to do something it would not do otherwise. Power relates to the ability of the stakeholder to disrupt organizational operations. Stakeholders who control essential resources or can form coalitions have strong power. Control over essential resources permits a stakeholder to disrupt organizational processes. For instance, employees can stop the production process or the delivery of goods and services. As noted earlier, the UPS drivers launched a strike that crippled the company's ability to deliver its primary service.

Coalition formation supplies power through numbers. As stakeholders join forces with one another, their power increases (Mitchell et al., 1997; Rowley, 1997). An example would be an activist group that persuades shareholders and customers to join its efforts to pressure an organization for change. The combination of activists, customers, and shareholders was instrumental in convincing Levi Strauss to close its production facilities in Myanmar. Activists persuaded customers and shareholders that facilities in Myanmar contributed to human rights violations there. In turn, customers and shareholders began to question Levi Strauss' involvement in Myanmar. Levi Strauss felt that the stigma of human rights abuse had become reason enough to leave

Myanmar (Cooper, 1997). Alone the activists have little power, but combined with shareholders and customers, they can exercise great power.

Stakeholder power is enhanced by the ability to take action against the organization. Stakeholders need resources (e.g., money) and skill in using communication channels if they are to put pressure on an organization (Ryan, 1991). Let us return to the NRDC's effort to ban Alar, a growth inhibitor that was used on apples. The NRDC had money to hire professional communicators to develop a major publicity campaign promoting the danger of Alar. The campaign raised awareness of Alar danger from 0% to 95% in less than a month (Center & Jackson, 1995). Money and publicity skills created the perception of Alar as a cancer threat to children.

Legitimacy is when actions are considered desirable, proper, or appropriate according to some system. A stakeholder threat is more serious when the concern is deemed legitimate by other stakeholders. Ignoring a legitimate concern makes the organization appear callous to the other stakeholders. Why doesn't the organization address this reasonable concern? Offending other stakeholders increases the risk of the threat spreading to additional organization-stakeholder relationships. Crisis managers should determine if other stakeholders will view the concern as legitimate. A crisis manager needs to know the values and social responsibility expectations of various stakeholder groups to assess a concern's legitimacy potential (Mitchell et al., 1997).

Willingness is the stakeholder's desire to confront the organization about the problem. A problem must be salient for the stakeholder, and its relationship to the organization must be weak. Salience prompts the stakeholder to take action. Why push a problem if it is unimportant? Once more, the Alar case illustrates the point. The NRDC considered Alar to be salient; it was the major concern of the NRDC at the time. Stakeholders are less likely to pursue a problem when they have a favorable relationship with the organization. The NRDC seemed to have no real relationship with the apple growers, the group affected most by the anti-Alar campaign. Documentation of the case makes no mention of the two sides ever meeting to discuss the concern prior to the launch of the NRDC's anti-Alar publicity campaign (Center & Jackson, 1995). A favorable relationship encourages both sides to seek a nonconfrontational approach to problem solving (Grunig & Repper, 1992).

Power, legitimacy, and willingness are related to the impact and likelihood criteria found in issues management and risk assessment. High power and legitimacy indicate a strong impact. The stakeholder can disrupt the organization and will be perceived by others as having valid (legitimate) reasons for doing so. Legitimacy and willingness suggest a strong likelihood of occurrence. Willingness increases the chance of a stakeholder taking action, and legitimacy increases the possibility of other stakeholders supporting the action. Each stakeholder threat can be rated in a 1 to 10 scale for power, legitimacy, and willingness. The highest-scoring threats should be tagged for immediate consideration.

APPLICATION POINT

Signal detection sounds easy to do. The intricacies of signal detection are learned by trying it. Here is an introduction to signal detection. First, select a specific organization and define its industry (e.g., steel manufacturing, automobile sales, etc.). Identify a list of potential issues, risks, and key stakeholders for the organization. Briefly explain why each issue, risk, and stakeholder should be on your list. Second, list the sources you would scan for potential prodromes. Your list of issues, risks, and stakeholders will help to guide your scanning. Be as specific as possible with your sources. For example, give specific television shows; do not just list "a television news shows." Also, identify the information collection tools you would use to extract information from the various sources. Third, develop precise evaluative dimensions for issues, risks, and stakeholder threats. List and define each of your dimensions.

From Scanning to Monitoring

The information analysis ends the scanning process and begins the monitoring process. Monitoring involves following the development of the prodromes. The crisis team continuously collects and analyzes information about the prodrome. The crisis team is looking for changes that indicate if the prodrome is becoming more or less likely to evolve into a crisis. The information sources, collection tools, and analytical criteria used in scanning are employed in monitoring. The key differences are a search for more detailed information and the continuous application of the search process in monitoring.

Crisis-Sensing Mechanism

The discussion of scanning and monitoring presupposes that issue, risk, and stakeholder information is received by the crisis team. Basically, signal detection involves knowing the sources of prodromal information, how to collect prodromal information, and how to evaluate prodromal information. Sources, collection tools, and evaluation criteria are the raw materials used to construct the crisis-sensing mechanism—the crisis radar and tracking system. No one crisis-sensing mechanism is right for all organizations; each organization has quirks that must be accommodated, but some basic ideas can be offered.

First, determine what information-sensing mechanisms already exist in your organization. Avoid re-creating the wheel. Review the issue management sources, risk sources, and stakeholder maps (the list of stakeholders associated with the organization) to see if they are comprehensive. New procedures should be developed only if key sources are being overlooked. For instance, if no efforts are being made to scan relevant activist groups, add that as a source. A similar review should be undertaken for information-gathering techniques. Pay particular attention to how information, such as publicity, is coded. A common weakness in information collection is a coding system that is too general and will miss important details contained in the information (Denbow & Culbertson, 1985).

An example illustrates the importance of details. Say a retail store tracks its media coverage by collecting and analyzing news stories that mention the organization. A general coding system might simply count the total number of positive and negative comments about the retail store. The analysis provides a global evaluation of the reputation—is the reputation favorable or unfavorable? No insight is provided into why the media image is favorable or unfavorable. A specific coding system might include the following categories: sales staff, customer service, selection, merchandise quality, value/pricing, store appearance, and parking. The retail store would have separate evaluations for the seven categories. Store managers would know the exact areas where the store's image was strong and where it needed improvement.

Second, the organization must establish mechanisms and procedures for funneling relevant information to the crisis team. A crisis team cannot process information it has not received or attend to warning signs it never encountered. The crisis team must receive the scanning information in a timely fashion and must carefully analyze the information for the warning signs. Various areas of the organization will be responsible for different pieces of internal information. Some of the organizational units involved in scanning include operations and manufacturing, marketing and sales, finance, human resources, legal, customer communications and satisfaction, environmental and safety engineering, public relations and public affairs, engineering, shipping and distribution, security, and quality assurance. The myriad of organizational units must send this information to the crisis team as soon as possible after they first receive and evaluate the information. Furthermore, the issues management unit or whatever unit(s) scans the environment must route the environmental information to the crisis team. The crisis team actually becomes the center of a large crisis-sensing mechanism. The crisis team must be a functioning unit that is integrated within the flow of organizational activities and information exchange.

Third, carefully develop the crisis team's evaluative criteria for prodromal information. This chapter provides general criteria for issues, risks, and stakeholder threats. Crisis teams may wish to add their own organization-specific evaluative criteria. The crisis team must determine which criteria it would like to use, develop additional criteria if need be, and determine precise definitions for the evaluative criteria. Without precise definitions, the crisis team will not be able to apply the evaluative criteria consistently. Finally, the crisis-sensing mechanism must be tested to determine if the various parts are integrated effectively. Running carefully selected control information through the system is one way to assess the integration effectiveness.

Conclusion

The first step in an ongoing approach to crisis management is to find potential crises before they find your organization. The crisis team must scan for crisis warning signs. Crisis scanning requires the crisis team to collect and analyze a wide array of environmental and internal data. But remember, the crisis team is not alone. Invariably, other organizational units (e.g., issues management, customer relations, or investor relations) can supply these data to the crisis team. The organization should formalize this information gathering into a crisis-sensing mechanism. Formalizing means setting procedures for funneling scanning information to the crisis team. Once received and analyzed, crisis teams move into the prevention phase, the subject of Chapter 4.

4

Crisis Prevention

Crisis prevention is the stage in which organizational members act on the warning signs or prodromes and try to curtail the onset of a crisis (Mitroff, 1986). Slightly different preventative measures are needed to stop issue, risk, and relationship prodromes from becoming crises. This chapter begins by outlining the basic structure of a crisis prevention system. Then, specific consideration is given to issues, risks, and relationships. Issues management and risk abatement have established programs, but little has been written about organization-stakeholder relationship building. As a result of this void, the majority of the chapter is devoted to relationship building and its ability to prevent crises.

Basic Crisis Prevention Process

An organization avoids crises by taking action on crisis warning signs and reducing its risk factors. Crisis managers must determine the exact nature of a crisis prevention program that will work in their organization. This section explains the basic process that undergirds any crisis prevention program.

The goal of a crisis prevention program is to defuse the crisis by attending to the warning signs and risks. The organization is taking actions it hopes will eliminate the potential crisis identified during the signal detection stage

(Pauchant & Mitroff, 1992). The crisis prevention program has two basic components: change and monitoring. The first component involves making changes that eliminate or reduce the likelihood of a warning sign becoming a crisis. Actions are taken to manage issues, reduce risks, and build relationships. A few examples will illustrate this point. The issues management unit learns of a proposal to tighten air quality standards. Action is taken to prevent the new regulation, thereby averting a possible plant closing. A safety review finds that workers are not following the unloading directions for hazardous chemicals. A refresher training course is offered along with new, stricter safety procedures regulating the unloading of chemicals. The risk of a hazardous materials accident is reduced. A number of complaints appear about leaks from a new deodorant. Customers are offered replacements, and steps are taken to prevent the container from leaking. A major conflict with customers is averted and the favorable relationship maintained.

Without monitoring, the organization does not know if the change was effective—has it reduced or eliminated the chance of a crisis? For example, an organization would want to know if the new safety procedures and policies made the workplace less hazardous. The only way to know if safety has improved is to monitor workplace behaviors. If workers are now engaging in safer behavior—fewer violations of safety procedures—then the safety changes are working. An organization must monitor its changes to determine if the warning signs and risks have become less acute. Never assume any change is for the better. Some changes produce no results, but others may intensify the warning signs or risks, thereby moving an organization closer to a crisis. Monitoring involves a regular review of any changes designed to reduce warning signs. The review determines the effectiveness of the changes and if any additional modifications are warranted (Pauchant & Mitroff, 1992). Crisis prevention is a two-step process designed to reduce or eliminate the possibility that a warning sign actually foretells a crisis.

Issues Management

After issues have been identified and analyzed, issue managers apply systematic procedures designed to influence the issue's resolution in a manner favorable to the organization. The approach is systematic. The Jones and Chase (1979) model is the dominant issues management model (Coombs, 1995b). The models provide crisis managers with directions on actions to take to prevent an issue from becoming a crisis and ways to evaluate the issues management effort.

Issues Management Process

Managing an issue involves attempts to shape how the issue is resolved. The idea is to have the issue resolved in a manner that is not a crisis. For instance, legislation is proposed that would threaten the financial viability of the railroad by making trucking companies more competitive with rail transportation. The issues management effort prevents a crisis by persuading Congress to reject the legislative proposal. Communication is used to influence an issue's resolution.

The Jones and Chase (1979) model is the classic issue identification, issue analysis, issue change strategy option, issue action program, and evaluation model familiar to most people involved in issues management. The issue action step centers on communicating the organization's position on the issue to stakeholders involved with the issue. Goals and objectives for the communication program are developed, followed by the selection of the means and resources needed to achieve the goals and objectives. Decisions are made about the specific messages to be communicated, when to communicate the messages, and the channels of communication to be used (Jones & Chase, 1979). Following through on the transportation example will clarify the issue action program. The railroad company decides that the goal is to prevent passage of the pro-trucking legislative proposal. Legislators, the media, and voters are the stakeholders to be targeted. The message centers on the danger to automobile drivers created by the pro-trucking legislation, and the message must be sent immediately because a vote will be held in a few months. Advertisements, publicity, and lobbying are the communication channels used.

Issues management can also involve changing the organization itself. Issue managers may decide that the best way to resolve an issue would be to correct or improve operating standards and plans. McDonald's illustrated this point when it abandoned the polystyrene "clamshell" burger boxes. Environmentalists had been complaining about the environmentally unfriendly clamshell packaging for years. McDonald's original plan was to win acceptance of the clamshell by emphasizing recycling. By recycling, McDonald's would eliminate the complaint that its packaging would clog landfills for hundreds of years. McDonald's was trying to change stakeholder attitudes. Consumers did not respond well to the early recycling tests. Instead, McDonald's abandoned the clamshell recycling campaign and simply ended their use (Snyder, 1991). McDonald's changed its procedures rather than trying to change its stakeholders opinions.

Issues management can be a form of crisis prevention when the issues management effort prevents an issue from developing its crisis potential (Grunig & Repper, 1992). A variety of communication tools are used in issues management, including advocacy advertising, direct lobbying, grassroots lobbying, letter writing, e-mail, Web pages, and publicity. The exact mix of communication strategies will depend on the stakeholders involved in the issues management effort and the current stage of the issue's life cycle.

Issues Management Evaluation

To evaluate the results of issues management, the final resolution of the issue is examined. Evaluation consists of comparing the actual resolution of the issue to the intended resolution of the issue. Success is measured by how closely the actual resolution matches the desired resolution (Jones & Chase, 1979). In our running example, the railroad issue managers were successful if the legislation was defeated—the actual and intended resolution were a match. Evaluation does not end with the issue's resolution. Issues are cyclical, and they have the potential to reappear. For example, the health care debate of the 1990s is much like the health care debate in the 1940s and 1950s. In the 1990s, President Clinton introduced the idea of health insurance for all Americans. The government would help to insure Americans who were currently uninsured for various reasons. In the 1940s and 1950s, President Truman advocated national health insurance. His idea was to make health insurance a reality for all Americans through government assistance. The national health insurance issue disappears for a while but never dies. The cyclical nature of issues means that the issue should be reexamined at least annually to see if it is gaining new momentum and might once again threaten the organization (Crable & Vibbert, 1985).

Risk Management

Risk management represents attempts to reduce the risks faced by an organization (Smallwood, 1995). Like crises, not all risks can be avoided or completely eliminated. Hence, risk management involves a number of strategies that vary in their crisis prevention potential. Two factors drive the use of risk management strategies. The first factor is cost. Risk managers use procedures such as risk balancing to compare the costs of the risk (e.g., costs of deaths, injuries, litigation, and property damage) to the costs of risks reduction (e.g., equipment and actual work needed to prevent or reduce the risk). Organizations may take no action when the costs of risk reduction outweigh the costs from the risk. However, ignoring risk can be a more costly move than anticipated. If stakeholders discover that their safety was sacrificed for profit, a different and much worse type of crisis erupts. The Pinto case taught Ford Motor Company the cost of privileging profit over people. Internal documents proved that Ford knew that the Pintos produced between 1970 and 1976 could explode in rear-end collisions. The crashes caused a differential housing bolt to puncture the gasoline tank and spark an explosion. Ford engineers tested a rubber bladder for the gasoline tank in 1970. The tests showed the bladder did correct the puncture problem. A cost-benefit analysis of the corrective action was performed. The corrections would cost $137 million, whereas the estimated injuries, deaths, and litigation would cost only $49.5 million (Birsch & Fielder, 1994). Ford executives decided it was more profitable to sell the faulty Pintos and litigate than to correct the flaw and protect customers. Ford knowingly placed its Pinto customers at risk of serious injury or death. Ford's decision was based on financial concerns, not customer safety concerns (Lerbinger, 1997; Levitt, 1997). The second factor is technical—can the risk actually be eliminated or reduced? No action is taken if there is no means for reducing the risk.

Risk Aversion Process

Risk management becomes crisis management when risk aversion (the avoidance or reduction of risk) is possible. Actions are taken to completely eliminate or reduce the risk to as low of a level as reasonably possible (Levitt, 1997). The use of dangerous chemicals in a manufacturing process will illustrate this point. If a nontoxic chemical can be substituted for a toxic chemical, a risk can be eliminated. If new handling procedures and equipment can reduce the risk of worker exposure to a toxic chemical, the risk is reduced. There are a wide variety of approaches for eliminating or reducing risk. The exact action taken by the organization to reduce the risk varies according to the actual risk (Lerbinger, 1997). The basic process involves determining if the risk aversion is possible and then implementing the risk aversion program.

Risk Aversion Evaluation

The evaluation of risk aversion is an ongoing concern. Periodic reviews of the risk are conducted to determine the effectiveness of the risk aversion program (Pauchant & Mitroff, 1992). Evaluation compares the level of risk before and after the risk aversion program is implemented. The review is continued to determine if the risk aversion program works over time. Was the risk reduction a statistical aberration, or is the lower level of risk maintained over the course of the risk aversion program? The risk must be monitored continually to ensure that the threat does not reemerge.

APPLICATION POINT

Risk monitoring can be challenging. Crisis managers have to find ways to measure the risk and to compare differences over time. For a specific organization, identify three important sources of risk. Explain how you would (a) monitor each of the risks and (b) determine whether your changes have been successful.

Relationship Building

Organizations are interdependent with their stakeholders. Therefore, organization-stakeholder relationships are naturally occurring. However, the quality of those relationships can vary greatly. Business and public relations experts agree that the quality of the organization-stakeholder relationship determines the effectiveness and success of an organization (e.g., Clarkson, 1995; Grunig, Grunig, & Ehling, 1992). The organization-stakeholder relationship has prominence within crisis management as well (e.g., Birch, 1994; Couretas, 1985; Fearn-Banks, 1996; Seitel, 1983). Unlike issues management and risk aversion, no models or procedures have been commonly accepted for developing stakeholder relationships. As a result, this section develops some guidelines for managing stakeholder relationships. By reviewing the various writings on organization-stakeholder relationships, it is possible to derive a list of elements important to constructing a favorable relationship and to understanding how to apply those elements. The end results are some actions that crisis managers can use to manage stakeholder relationships and thereby prevent crises.

Elements of a Favorable
Organization-Stakeholder Relationship

Three central elements emerge from the writings about the nature of organization-stakeholder relationships: staying close, credibility, and meeting expectations. Each of these elements will be explained along with a discussion of their value and application to crisis management.

Staying Close

Business guru Tom Peters has been preaching for years the need to stay close to one's customers (Peters, 1994). Staying close allows an organization to anticipate and fulfill the needs of the customer. As Grunig (1992) notes, staying close should be applied to all stakeholders, not just to the customers. Staying close allows the organization and the stakeholders to better understand one another (Grunig & Grunig, 1992). Ideally, the organization and the stakeholders become involved in a dialogue through which mutual understanding becomes mutual respect. Ultimately, mutual understanding should result in both parties forming positive perceptions of one another (Grunig, 1992). Two-way communication with stakeholders enhances the reputation of the organization. Experts in integrated marketing communication (IMC) concur with the idea that dialogue builds positive relationships. "Interactive communication" is a critical feature of the IMC synergy model. Interactive communication is two-way in nature—it is a dialogue. It is through interactive communication that organization-stakeholder relationships are built (Moriarity, 1994). The mutual understanding and respect derived from dialogues help organizations to cultivate a favorable reputation with stakeholders.

Grunig and Repper (1992) consider relationship building to be a variant of signal detection. Staying close to stakeholders allows organizations to identify problems early on and to prevent these problems from developing into issues. A problem occurs when something is perceived to be lacking in a situation, and an issue involves conflict because there is a public point of contention. When a problem goes unaddressed, it festers; conflict between the organization and stakeholder intensifies; and the problem grows into an issue. Conflict escalation can be avoided by dealing with the problem when it is detected at an earlier stage. The early detection and resolution of problems facilitate the development of more harmonious organization-stakeholder relationships (Grunig & Repper, 1992). A positive relationship facilitates the identification and prevention of would-be crises.

The earlier discussion of the Nike flaming logo case illustrates the advantages of early detecting and intervention. The flaming logo looked like the word *Allah* in Arabic and offended Muslims. Nike had received negative feedback on the shoe's prototype the year before but still released the shoe. In June 1997, Nike took actions, including (a) apologizing to the Islamic community for inadvertently offending them, (b) a global recall of original sales samples, (c) diverting all commercial shipments away from Islamic markets, (d) discontinuing all models with the offensive logo, and (e) pulling back all remaining shoes from distribution centers.

The changes at Nike were in response to a mid-March public protest by the Council on American Islamic Relations (CAIR). Nike was first alerted to the problem in September 1996. An Islamic distributor pointed out that the logo on the prototype shoe looked like the Arabic version of "Allah" and that it would be offensive to the Muslim community. Some redesign of the writing was made, but CAIR still felt that the design looked too much like Allah ("Muslim Concerns," 1997). The design problem became an issue when CAIR took the protest public. Had Nike dropped the design or properly altered the design at the first hint of a problem, the "Allah" recall would not have become an issue. Staying close to stakeholders allows crisis managers to identify and resolve problems in the organization-stakeholder relationship that could evolve into crises.

Organizational Credibility

Credibility is a concept that is used in persuasion and is defined as the receiver's attitude toward the communicator. For crisis management, the organization is the communicator and the stakeholders are the receivers. Credibility is a very important concept because it has a significant effect on the persuasiveness of a message (McCroskey, 1997). Research has proven that credibility can be divided into two components, expertise and trustworthiness. Expertise is the communicator's knowledge about the subject. An expert organization will appear to be competent, capable, and effective (Kouzes & Posner, 1993). Trustworthiness is the communicator's goodwill toward or concern for the receivers. A trustworthy organization is truthful and ethical, and it considers the impact of its actions on stakeholders when making decisions (Allen & Caillouet, 1994; Kouzes & Posner, 1993).

Although not referred to directly, credibility is actually an underlying theme in much of the crisis management literature. Two common refrains noted by crisis experts are that an organization must establish control during a crisis and show compassion during a crisis (e.g., Carney & Jorden, 1993; Frank, 1994; Sen & Egelhoff, 1991). When we examine what is meant by control and compassion, we find a strong similarity to the expertise and trustworthiness dimensions of credibility. Control includes having accurate and complete information about the crisis (Bergman, 1994; Caruba, 1994; Kempner, 1995). Having information shows that the organization is an expert about the crisis. Compassion means showing concern and sensitivity for those affected by the crisis (Higbee, 1992; Mitchell, 1986). Compassion is consistent with trustworthiness. We trust those who seem to have our own best interests in mind. Thus, crisis experts have indirectly argued the importance of credibility during crisis management.

Credibility is a dynamic, not a static, concept. Being dynamic means credibility is best examined over time. Examining credibility over time results in three types of credibility existing: initial, derived, and terminal. *Initial credibility* is the credibility the communicator has before he or she speaks. *Derived credibility* is the credibility produced by the communicator's message. *Terminal credibility* is the credibility after the communicator has spoken and represents a combination of initial and derived credibility (McCroskey, 1997). The different types of credibility hold implications for crisis managers. An organization that lacks initial credibility must work especially hard during a crisis to build credibility—an organization must facilitate the development of derived credibility. Crisis experts acknowledge that building credibility during a crisis is a very difficult task (Fearn-Banks, 1996). Although difficult, an organization can build derived credibility. Gerber's 1986 bout with concerns over glass in its baby food is an example of building derived credibility.

In 1986, numerous press reports began to appear that claimed glass had been found in baby food manufactured by Gerber. Consumer groups wanted the products recalled and the faulty manufacturing system repaired. Gerber refused to recall the products and countered that there were no problems with the manufacturing process. Gerber built its derived credibility by finding experts who supported its position. The Food and Drug Administration and the health departments of numerous states reported that they had investigated the claims and found no glass in the products and had deemed the manufacturing process safe. Gerber seemed successful in building derived credibility as it lost only a 1% market share that it quickly regained (Cook & Miller,

1986; Strnad, 1986). Had Gerber not built its credibility, the losses would have been much worse. Who would buy baby food they did not believe was safe? Lack of initial credibility and a failure to build derived credibility mean that the organization will lack terminal credibility. The failure to establish terminal credibility is problematic. Stakeholders will be less likely to believe messages sent by an organization when it has low terminal credibility.

Believability is essential during any type of crisis event because there always can be competing interpretations of a crisis. For this reason, crisis experts repeatedly emphasize that an organization must get its side of the story or version of the crisis out quickly (e.g., Heath, 1994; Kempner, 1995). However, this advice has a hidden premise—it is assumed that stakeholders will believe what the organization has to say. The importance of believability is heightened when the crisis hinges on the stakeholders choosing between competing versions of the crisis story. In some crises, the version of the crisis story that the stakeholders accept will determine the success of the crisis management effort and affect the amount of damage inflicted by the crisis. Challenges and rumors are two types of crises that rest on the selection of competing crisis stories (Lerbinger, 1997). A closer look at challenges and rumors will clarify the importance of credibility to crisis management.

Challenges occur when a stakeholder calls an organization's actions into question. The stakeholder claims that the organization is acting in ways that are inappropriate. Other stakeholders must decide whether to accept the claim of wrongdoing or to accept the organization's claim that its actions are appropriate (Lerbinger, 1997). Challenges are marked by ambiguity, and there are some reasons why both sides may be correct. The ambiguity stems from the challenges being based either on morals or questions of product and service quality. A moral challenge is tied to some set of moral principles such as a code of conduct. The Sullivan Principles, which governed investment in South Africa before apartheid was repealed, and the United Nations' declaration of human rights are examples of such codes. A moral challenge does not involve the violation of any law or regulation. What is violated is a set of standards some stakeholders believe to be appropriate behavior. Some actual examples include not buying furs because of the inhumane treatment of animals or not buying oil from Nigeria because of the Nigerian government's human rights abuses. The potential for a moral challenge is great because the world is composed of many diverse groups with often conflicting views of what is appropriate conduct. During a moral challenge, stakeholders will support the side that is the most believable or credible.

A quality of product and service challenge derives its ambiguity from how the data that measure quality are interpreted or from competing data sets that lead to different conclusions about the product and service quality. The Audi 5000 sudden acceleration case exemplifies the ambiguity that can be associated with interpreting quality data. For a number of years, Audi 5000 drivers reported that the car would suddenly jump into gear and run. Sometimes there were deadly consequences when people were unlucky enough to be in the vehicle's path at the time of the jump. Many customers defined the situation as a quality problem, a fault in the design of the Audi 5000's transmission system. Audi maintained there was no reliable evidence that the transmission was faulty. Instead, Audi blamed the incidents on bad drivers. No definitive evidence supported either story; it all depended on how one interpreted the events. Eventually, the 5000 was recalled and an antilocking device installed. Audi still maintained there was no problem, but stakeholders, including potential car buyers, found the Audi customers to have the more believable and credible story (Versical, 1987). Unless there is a government action such as a recall or a jury decision in a lawsuit, challenges based on quality are resolved by stakeholders selecting the story they feel comes from the most credible source.

Rumors represent another form of crisis in which believability is essential. A rumor occurs when a untruthful statement about your organization is circulated. The Snapple Beverage Company was hit by rumors that it supported the Ku Klux Klan and that the label on its popular ice tea drink depicted a slave ship. The rumor was centered in San Francisco, and Snapple launched a costly media campaign to combat the rumor. The origin of the rumor seemed to be the kosher mark that Snapple, like hundreds of other companies, placed on its bottles (Gellene, 1993). The charges were false, and the organization spent thousands of dollars to correct the lies. Rumor experts recommend that organizations respond immediately to rumors by stating that the information is untrue and unjust (Gross, 1990). Once more, a premium is placed on the credibility and believability of the organization. Defusing a rumor requires that the organization be perceived as a credible channel of information—the stakeholders must believe the organization is a source of accurate information. The organization must be more credible than the rumor.

Credibility is a vital component of the stakeholder's attitude toward the organization. The benefit of credibility is that it increases the believability of an organization's message. The more credible the organization, the more likely stakeholders are to believe and accept the organization's definition of the crisis—believe the organization's side of the story. A second characteristic of a favorable precrisis organization-stakeholder relationship would be stakeholders viewing the organization as credible.

Meeting Expectations

Some business theorists place a great deal of importance on an organization maintaining its legitimacy (Bediean, 1989; Orru, Biggart, & Hamilton, 1991). An organization is considered to be legitimate when it conforms to the expectations of its stakeholders. Legitimate organizations avoid criticism, are viewed as good, and receive support from stakeholders. Conversely, failure to meet expectations leads to criticism and conflict with stakeholders (Finet, 1994). Corporate executives even argue that legitimacy is more important to an organization's success than is technical efficiency (Allen & Caillouet, 1994). Legitimacy implies a favorable relationship. Stakeholders accept the organization as good and support it. A third characteristic of a favorable precrisis organization-stakeholder relationship would be that the stakeholders feel their expectations are being met.

In summary, features of a favorable organization-stakeholder relationship include (a) the organization and stakeholders engage in two-way communication on a regular basis, (b) mutual understanding and respect, (c) the organization is viewed as competent and capable of performing its tasks, (d) the organization is viewed as truthful and ethical, (e) the organization is considered to have a right to operate, (f) the organization understands the performance expectations held by its various stakeholders, (g) the organization demonstrates that it is concerned about its stakeholders, and (h) the organization meets most stakeholder performance expectations.

Benefits

The three central characteristics of a favorable precrisis organization-stakeholder relationship are interrelated. This interrelatedness becomes more evident when we examine the overall value of a favorable precrisis relationship and the actions crisis managers can take to facilitate the development of a favorable precrisis relationship. To more completely understand and appreciate the interconnectedness, we need to explore why a favorable organization-stakeholder relationship is believed to help during a crisis.

A theme that connects staying close, credibility, and expectations is the organization's reputation. An organization's reputation is the product of stakeholders' perceptions of what it does and says (Crable & Vibbert, 1986). Staying close cultivates a favorable organizational reputation through mutual understanding and the development of mutual respect (Gonzalez- Herrero & Pratt, 1996). Meeting expectations also builds mutual respect. When an organization meets stakeholder expectations, it signals to the stakeholder that it values and respects the concerns of that stakeholder group. Credibility has been used as a broad measure of reputation (Denbow & Culbertson, 1985). Others consider credibility to be one of the building blocks of reputation (Herbig, Milewicz, & Golden, 1994). Being credible indicates a favorable organization-stakeholder relationship because the organization is perceived as expert and trustworthy, two rather positive traits. A favorable precrisis relationship reflects a favorable organizational reputation.

A reputation is derived from experiences with the organization, the relational history with stakeholders. Stakeholders reflect on their experiences to determine if the organizational reputation is favorable or unfavorable (Botan, 1993; Boulding, 1977). Stakeholders evaluate each interaction with an organization. Herbig et al. (1994) referred to the organization-stakeholder interactions as credibility transactions. A credibility transaction is an individual instance of when an organization's stated intentions are matched to its actions—an evaluation of whether an organization lived up to its words. A reputation is the sum of the credibility transactions between an organization and a stakeholder. Positive credibility transactions (living up to one's word) lead to favorable reputations (Herbig et al., 1994). Hence, if an organization consistently does what it tells a stakeholder group that it will do, the organization builds a favorable reputation (Baskin & Aronoff, 1988). Whatever we choose to call them, stakeholder experiences with the organization are what constitute the organization-stakeholder relationship. Stakeholders evaluate each organization based on their experiences with it. The organization's reputation is a reflection of the organization-stakeholder relationship. But how does all of this help the crisis manager?

The organizational reputation can be likened to a bank account. A favorable reputation builds up the account, whereas a crisis subtracts from the account. A strong account suffers little from the withdrawals of a crisis. A favorable precrisis reputation serves to protect an organization from the reputational damage generated by a crisis. A reputation is a very stable concept; it is hard to change once people form a strong reputation. A favorable precrisis relationship should lead to a strong, favorable reputation for the organization. Stakeholders even ignore contradictory information about reputations (Balzer & Sulsky, 1992; Boulding, 1977; Nisbett & Wilson, 1977). An organization with a favorable reputation will experience stakeholders ignoring bad news about the organization because stakeholders are unlikely to believe that a good organization did anything bad. Crises can be one of the forms of bad news that is deflected by a strong reputation.

The disbelief gives the organization the benefit of doubt during the initial phases of a crisis. The benefit of the doubt provides two advantages to an organization in crisis. First, it supplies a buffer against people assuming the worst. In a crisis, the worst is when stakeholders believe the organization is responsible for the crisis. The stronger the perceptions of organizational responsibility for a crisis, the more reputational damage the crisis inflicts on the organization (Coombs & Holladay, 1996). Although most people are quick to believe the worst about organizations, a favorable reputation leads stakeholders to believe the best. In turn, this means the stakeholders should not jump to negative conclusions about the crisis. This position would then be reevaluated once the facts about the crisis begin to emerge.

Second, a favorable reputation affords protection from the negative speculation that crises often produce. Negative speculation refers to the nonexpert opinions that often fill the information void created by a crisis. Organizations are wise to respond immediately to prevent this void. However, negative speculation may come quicker than the facts during a crisis (Carney & Jorden, 1993). The negative speculation feeds into people's willingness to assume the worst about organizations, particularly corporations. The favorable reputation counters the negative speculation and the willingness to believe the worst. A favorable reputation should lead stakeholders to discount the negative speculation and to believe the best about an organization until that belief is proven to be unfounded. The stakeholders are predisposed to wait to hear the organization's side of the story before drawing conclusions about the crisis. A strong, favorable, precrisis organization-stakeholder relationship shields the organization from undue reputational harm and makes it easier for the organization to deliver its side of the story.

Building Favorable Relationships

Because favorable organization-stakeholder relationships are valuable, crisis managers should want to build just such a relationship. Understanding what goes into a favorable relationship provides the foundation for explaining how each one can be constructed. The two basic elements for building a favorable organization-stakeholder relationship are regular, two-way communication and matching an organization's words to its deeds.

Staying close involves regular, two-way communication with stakeholders. The communication must be regular because the organization and the stakeholders change. Understanding is lost if the parties drift out of contact and fail to appreciate even minor changes in each party. Communication must be two-way if both parties are to receive information about the other. One-way communication privileges the sending party and does not facilitate mutual understanding (Grunig, 1992). Furthermore, mutual understanding allows organizations to identify and shape stakeholder expectations. By talking with stakeholders, an organization learns what its expectations are. When these expectations are unrealistic, the organization can engage in a dialogue with the stakeholders. The goal of this dialogue is to develop a new set of expectations that both parties can agree on—a set of realistic expectations (Finet, 1994). Prior to any crisis, the organization should develop a systematic program for regular, two-way communication with key stakeholders to promote mutual understanding.

Credibility also requires regular contact. Credibility is built through action; an organization proves it can make good on its words. Over time, credibility is earned as the organization proves to stakeholders that it does what it says it will do (Kouzes & Posner, 1993). Organizational credibility with stakeholders is a function of repeated, honest dealings with the stakeholders (e.g., Baskin & Aronoff, 1988). Legitimacy helps develop credibility. Legitimacy requires that an organization meet the expectations of stakeholders. Moreover, organizations must communicate these met expectations to the stakeholders. Legitimacy results when actions match words; an organization proves it is meeting expectations. Failure to meet expectations results in a loss of legitimacy and other problems for the organization (Allen & Caillouet, 1994). Both credibility and legitimacy involve making good on organizational promises to stakeholders. Two-way communication allows an organization to keep track of its promises to stakeholders and evaluate whether those promises have been met.

Development and maintenance of a two-way communication system with stakeholders result in what I term the *stakeholder communication network*. The stakeholder communication network is a list of organizational stakeholders, organizational contact points for those stakeholders, and the primary people in the organization responsible for communicating with each stakeholder. Development requires that key stakeholders be identified, contact people for the stakeholders be located, and the most effective means of communicating with these stakeholders be specified. Organizations should have a map of their key stakeholders because organizational survival depends on these stakeholders (Grunig, 1992). A stakeholder map is simply a list of all the publics that could affect or be affected by an organization. Stakeholder analysis should be a part of the crisis team's crisis information database. A list of stakeholders is useless unless it provides the requisite contact information. Organizational members must know (a) who to contact in the stakeholder group when seeking to engage in two-way communication and (b) the most effective channels for reaching them. Who to contact means identifying the opinion leaders and or spokespersons for various stakeholder groups. This may be as simple as keeping track of who from the stakeholder group contacts the organization or may require a little research. Just as the public relations practitioners develop and revise a list of media contacts, crisis managers should have up-to-date lists of contacts for all stakeholders.

Once established, the stakeholder communication network must be maintained. Maintenance involves meeting regularly, identifying expectations, and checking promise fulfillment. The stakeholder communication network is a lifetime commitment. The system must be kept functional for the life of the organization if it is to be effective. Functional means that there is a regular two-way flow of information between the organization and the stakeholders. Neglect of the stakeholder communication system leads to problems. Bob Evans Farms, Inc. discovered this fact when it drifted out of two-way communication with investors. Bob Evans lapsed into a limited one-way communication routine whereby it only sent brief information to investors. The poor communication system led to a drop in earnings and lagging stock prices, the early signs of a financial crisis. The potential crisis was averted when Bob Evans dedicated itself to regular, two-way communication with investors. The improved relationship eliminated the earnings and stock price prodromes (Center & Jackson, 1995).

The use of regular, two-way communication helps an organization to determine the expectations of its stakeholders. By talking with stakeholders, the organization learns what standards of performance (expectations) the stakeholders are using to evaluate the organization, and stakeholders learn if the organization is meeting their expectations. Moreover, by learning more about the organization, the stakeholders may modify their own expectations to be more consistent with what the organization can actually deliver. Part of communication is making promises—saying what the organization will do. Unlike politicians, an organization should not forget its promises, especially those related to expectations of organizational performance. Stakeholders will watch to determine if the organization delivers on its words. Only by developing a history of honoring its promises can an organization establish credibility and legitimacy with its stakeholders.

APPLICATION POINT

Crisis managers must know the channels available for reaching their stakeholders if they are to stay close. For a specific organization, list the key stakeholders and potential communication channels available for reaching each stakeholder. Then, rate each communication channel for two-way communication potential—the degree to which the communication channel facilitates interaction. Feedback (how quickly people can respond to a message) and interpersonal warmth (ability to communicate interpersonal warmth) are important considerations when evaluating a channel's two-way communication potential.

Organization-Stakeholder Relationship Evaluation

Some social responsibility experts have established a scorecard that corporations use to evaluate their social performance. The scorecard tracks what the organization is doing to meet each stakeholder's expectations for the organization's performance (Clarkson, 1991; Fombrun & Shanley, 1990). Sample scorecard items include contributions to charity, development of nonpolluting products, equal opportunity employment, creating foundations, and placing women and minority members on boards (Fombrun & Shanley, 1990). Clarkson (1991, 1995) has developed one of the most extensive social performance evaluation systems with his ETHIDEX. ETHIDEX stores, organizes, and provides an evaluation system for analyzing social performance. The system organizes information by stakeholder group. For instance, the shareholder section contains information on general policies, shareholder communication and complaints, shareholder advocacy, shareholder rights, and other shareholder issues (Clarkson, 1991). Social performance is evaluated on a 4-point scale: 1 = reactive, deny responsibility—do less than required; 2 = defensive, admit responsibility but fight it—do the least that is required; 3 = accommodative, accept responsibility—do all that is required; and 4 = proactive, anticipate responsibility—do more than is required (Clarkson, 1995). This evaluative system indicates if the organization fails to meet, meets, or exceeds stakeholder expectations for various aspects of social performance. The ETHIDEX is one of many systems an organization can use to evaluate its social performance. Any scorecard system seeks to determine whether an organization's words match its actions and if it is meeting stakeholder expectations.

The social responsibility scorecards demonstrate that organizations can and do monitor their stakeholder interactions. Scorecards can be extended to monitor all stakeholder interactions and not just those limited to social performance. Integrated marketing communication advocates argue for keeping databases to track communication with stakeholders. By combining a scorecard and the communication tracking database, the organization can develop a system for monitoring and evaluating stakeholder relationships. Evaluation is the key. Organizations must know where the relationship stands, why it is in that state, and how it might be improved. Monitoring provides the information needed to evaluate the relationship.

The organization-stakeholder evaluation system combines objective data with subjective stakeholder evaluations as well as a means of tracking messages. Section one contains the objective data—it records the organization's actual financial performance and the actions taken to meet social needs. The financial and social sections are broad and should reflect the nature of the organization. Thus, there can be no set checklist for financial and social performance. Section one can be long or short depending on the financial statistics and social activities of the organization. The performance of these objective factors can be rated using the four categories from the ETHIDEX system—reactive, defensive, accommodative, and proactive. The organization's evaluation of its own performance must then be compared against the perceptions of stakeholders, section two.

Reputational research tells us that organizations and stakeholders do not always see issues or actions in the same manner (Crable & Vibbert, 1986). An organization can view itself as an environmental champion, whereas stakeholders perceive it as a polluter. Stakeholders would be asked to rate the organization on its dominant performance expectations and the overall quality of the organization-stakeholder relationship. The individual dominant performance expectations provide details about the relationship. The organization learns more precisely why a relationship is weak or strong. For instance, stakeholders might expect an organization to buy supplies locally, exceed clean air and water standards, offer day care to its workers, and be involved in the social fabric of the community. The organization would identify the dominant performance expectations through formative research with each stakeholder group. Typically this would involve focus group research because the goal is to discover the expectations held by the stakeholders.

Finally, the organization would track the messages sent to the stakeholders. The basic tracking information includes data, channel(s), and the unit(s) responsible for the message. Goals and actual messages reflect the strategic aspect of messages. Goals indicate the purpose of the communication—what the organization was trying to achieve (Barton, 1993). The actual message includes an analysis of any promises made or actions taken to deliver on promises. Because actions must support the organization's words, crisis managers should track performance to see if the organization is living up to its words. Crisis managers will need to adapt the system to meet the specific needs of their organizations. Whatever the composition of the system, the organization-stakeholder relationship should be reviewed at least annually to determine how the organization is doing in terms of meeting expectations and fulfilling promises.

APPLICATION POINT

This section provides the basic components of the organization-stakeholder relationship evaluation form. Every organization must develop the form to fit its own characteristics and needs. For a specific organization, construct an organization-stakeholder relationship evaluation form. Explain why each element is on the form—how does the information help you to understand and evaluate the organization-stakeholder relationship?

Conclusion

Crisis management is best when it includes avoiding or preventing crises. Issues management, risk management/aversion, and relationship building can all be used to avoid crises or at least their most dire consequences. Some issues can evolve into crises. Issues management can be used to prevent such crises. All risks have the potential of becoming crises. Risk aversion is used to lessen the chance of a risk becoming a crisis. A favorable organization-stakeholder relationship will identify problems early on and seek to resolve the problems. By understanding and working with one another, the organization and its stakeholders can resolve problems early on before they escalate into crises. For example, customer complaints can be corrected before the customers become outraged and publicly protest about a product or service. To assist crisis management efforts, the means of facilitating a favorable organization-stakeholder relationship were outlined in this chapter. This chapter also featured benefits that could be derived from building strong relationships.

A crisis prevention program is a valuable part of the crisis management process. The crisis team uses the warning signs from signal detection to target situations that could become crises. The crisis team then takes actions designed to eliminate or reduce the likelihood of the warning signs developing into crises. Unfortunately, organizational politics can block efforts to reduce risks. Chapter 6 offers suggestions for combating resistance to preventative actions. Ideally, the crisis team must remember to monitor its corrective actions on a regular basis to determine if the preventative actions had the desired effect. However, an organization cannot count on avoiding all crises. Hence, the need remains for crisis preparation, the subject of Chapter 5.

5

Crisis Preparation

Collecting the information about potential crises provides a foundation for crisis preparation. During crisis preparation, an organization readies itself for the inevitable crises that will befall it. Organizations should not fall victim to hubris and assume that their preventative measures will protect them from harm. All organizations should prepare to handle crises by addressing six concerns: diagnosing vulnerabilities, assessing crisis types, selecting and training the crisis team, selecting and training the spokesperson, developing the crisis management plan (CMP), and reviewing the communication system.

Diagnosing Crisis Vulnerabilities

As noted at the beginning of this book, a vast array of potential crises can happen to an organization. However, every organization will have specific crisis vulnerabilities (Fink, 1986). These vulnerabilities are a function of the organization's industry, size, location, operations, personnel, and risk factors. For example, a hotel must ensure the safety of hundreds of people who are in an unfamiliar building, whereas food producers run the risk of contamination that poisons their customers. Different types of organizations are prone to different types of crises. Crisis managers must identify the crises for which their organizations are most vulnerable. Vulnerabilities affect the development of the CMP (Pauchant & Mitroff, 1992).

Vulnerabilities typically are assessed using a combination of the likelihood of occurrence and severity of damage dimensions. Crisis managers start by listing all possible crises that could affect an organization. The list of potential crises can result from brainstorming by the crisis management team (CMT) or an assessment done by a consultant (Barton, 1993). Once a final list of potential crises is developed, each crisis should be assessed. A common approach is to rate each crisis from 1 to 10 (with 10 being the strongest score) for likelihood and impact (Fink, 1986). Likelihood represents the odds that the crisis might happen. Impact is the amount of damage a crisis can inflict on an organization. The crisis manager then multiplies the likelihood and impact ratings to establish a final crisis vulnerability score. The higher the score, the greater the potential damage that crisis can generate (Barton, 1993; Fink, 1986). Crisis managers should focus their attention on crises that have the highest crisis vulnerability score. Summaries of the crisis assessments are often included in the CMP.

Crisis Types

The list of potential crises for organizations is extremely long. Crises include accidents, activist actions, boycotts, earthquakes, explosions, chemical leaks, rumors, deaths, fire, lawsuits, sexual harassment, product recalls, strikes, terrorism, and whistle-blowing, to name but a few (Fearn-Banks, 1996; Pauchant & Mitroff, 1992). There is a point to the laundry list of crises—organizations face different threats, not just one, when it comes to crises. Different crises can necessitate the use of different crisis team members and an emphasis on different stakeholders, as well as warrant different crisis communication strategies. For instance, a product recall is not the same as a rumor. A product recall requires the organization to tell consumers how to return the product and to inform shareholders of the financial impact of the recall. A rumor requires a response designed to present the truth to consumers and to stop the source of the rumor.

Although crises possess different characteristics, they tend to cluster into identifiable types (Coombs, Hazleton, Holladay, & Chandler, 1995). Although an organization cannot prepare a CMP for every single crisis, it can prepare CMPs for the major types of crises it may face. A variety of crisis typologies can be found in the crisis writings (e.g., Egelhoff & Sen, 1992; Lerbinger, 1997; Marcus & Goodman, 1991; Newsom et al., 1996; Pearson

& Mitroff, 1993). These typologies have been synthesized into one master list.

Natural disasters: when an organization is damaged as a result of the weather or "acts of God." Sample natural disasters include earthquakes, tornadoes, floods, hurricanes, and bad storms (Coombs et al., 1995; Egelhoff & Sen, 1992; Fearn-Banks, 1996; Lerbinger, 1997).

Malevolence: when some outside actor or opponent employs extreme tactics to express anger toward the organization or to force the organization to change. Sample malevolence crises include product tampering, kidnapping, malicious rumors, terrorism, and espionage (Coombs et al., 1995; Egelhoff & Sen, 1992; Fearn-Banks, 1996; Lerbinger, 1997; Pauchant & Mitroff, 1992).

Technical breakdowns: when the technology used or supplied by the organization fails or breaks down. Sample technical breakdowns include industrial accidents, software failures, and product recalls that result from technical problems (Lerbinger, 1997; Pauchant & Mitroff, 1992).

Human breakdowns: when human error causes disruptions. Sample human breakdowns include industrial accidents and product recalls caused by human error (Coombs et al., 1995; Marcus & Goodman, 1991).

Challenges: when the organization is confronted by discontented stakeholders. The stakeholders challenge the organization because they believe it is operating in an inappropriate manner—does not meet their expectations. Sample confrontations include boycotts, strikes, lawsuits, government penalties, and protests (Lerbinger, 1997; Pauchant & Mitroff, 1992).

Megadamage: when an accident creates significant environmental damage. Sample megadamage includes oil spills and radioactive contamination (Fearn-Banks, 1996; Pauchant & Mitroff, 1992). Megadamage is caused by either technical or human breakdowns or both.

Organizational misdeeds: when management takes actions it knows will harm or place stakeholders at risk for harm without adequate precautions. These acts serve to discredit or disgrace the organization in some way. Sample organizational misdeeds include favoring short-term economic gain over social values, deliberate deception of stakeholders, and amoral or illegal acts by management (Lerbinger, 1997; Marcus & Goodman, 1991).

Workplace violence: when an employee or former employee commits violence against other employees on organizational grounds. Sample workplace violence includes killing or injuring coworkers (Coombs et al., 1995; Fearn-Banks, 1996).

Rumors: when false information is spread about an organization or its products. The false information hurts the organization's reputation by putting the organization in a unfavorable light. Sample rumors includes linking the organization to radical groups or stories that their products are contaminated (Fearn-Banks, 1996; Gross, 1990).

The organizational vulnerability and crisis types can help crisis managers to construct their crisis portfolios—the specific crises that could affect an organization. First, organize the list of potential crises by crisis type. Second, select at least one crisis from each crisis type. Select the crises with the highest vulnerability rating. The highest-rated crisis in each crisis type becomes part of the crisis portfolio. Third, develop variations of the CMP for each crisis in the portfolio. The logic is simple; an organization cannot prepare plans for every individual crisis, but it can prepare plans for each crisis type. Because of the similarities of the crises within each type, one CMP can be used to address any crisis within a particular crisis type (Pauchant & Mitroff, 1992). The crisis portfolio prepares an organization to cope with a wide array of crises.

APPLICATION POINT

For a specific organization, construct a crisis portfolio. To create the portfolio you must (a) list the potential crises the organization faces, (b) group the crises by crisis type, and (c) evaluate the likelihood and impact of each crisis. It is best to do this exercise in a group—a matrix of all relevant disciplines. Brainstorming will help to create a thorough list of potential crises. Reaching agreement on the evaluations will help to clarify the decision-making process behind the task.

APPLICATION POINT

Before reading the CMT section, complete the following tasks. First, list the functional areas you would want to have on a CMT. A functional area is just a unit in an organization such as research and development, production, or sales. Note why you included each functional area—what each area can contribute to the CMT. Second, list the characteristics you feel are important for CMT members—what type of person you want on your CMT. Explain why each characteristic could help the CMT. After reading the CMT section, compare your answers to points presented in the book. How were your lists similar or different from the ones presented in the chapter?

Crisis Management Teams

The CMT is a cross-functional group of people in the organization who have been designated to handle any crises. Typically, the CMT is responsible for (a) creating the CMP, (b) enacting the CMP, and (c) dealing with any problems not covered in the CMP. The CMT crafts the crisis management plan after thoroughly researching an organization's vulnerabilities. The CMP planning includes anticipating the most likely crises to befall an organization (Pauchant & Mitroff, 1992). To develop the crisis plan, the crisis team needs the information about different crisis types and all information about potential crises (scanning) and actions being taken to prevent crises (prevention). Any background information relevant to crises is helpful when the crisis team is writing the CMP.

A second CMT responsibility is to enact the CMP during simulated or real crises. CMPs must be tested to see if they work. The CMPs are tested by running the entire organization, departments, or just the crisis team through drills and simulations. The simulations help to discover any holes in the CMP or weaknesses in the CMT (Pauchant & Mitroff, 1992; Regester, 1989). The CMTs are responsible for implementing the CMP during real crises as well. We must remember that CMPs are contingency plans. This means that a CMT must be able to adapt to situational experiences and not just mindlessly follow a CMP (Fink, 1986; Littlejohn, 1983). This brings us to the third major responsibility of the CMT, dealing with factors not covered in the CMP. It is impossible for a CMP to anticipate all possible contingencies in every crisis. During an actual crisis, the CMT must be able to provide counsel on and to resolve issues not dealt with in the CMP (Barton, 1993; Regester, 1989). It falls to the CMT to make the necessary decisions when a crisis presents a challenge not covered in the CMP.

Development of an effective CMT is essential to the crisis management process. The best CMP is worthless if the CMT cannot fulfill its crisis duties (Wilson & Patterson, 1987). An effective CMT is developed through careful selection and training. Selection involves choosing the people best suited for the tasks, whereas training helps people to improve skills and become more proficient at performing tasks (Goldstein, 1993). Careful selection and training produce more effective workers; that is why organizations spend millions of dollars a year on each.

Task Analysis

The key to selection and training is the identification of the characteristics (knowledge, skills, and traits) people need to perform their jobs (Goldstein, 1993). Task analysis is the technical term for identifying the key characteristics needed for job performance. A task analysis of crisis management should isolate the characteristics required by crisis team members. Once tasks are identified, the knowledge, skills, and traits needed to perform each task should be determined. Through interviews with crisis managers and an analysis of crisis management writings, four specific tasks were isolated: group decision making, functioning as a team, enacting the CMP, and listening (Coombs & Chandler, 1996). Table 5.1 summarizes the task analysis.

Very little information exists about the characteristics of crisis team members. The discussions of personal characteristics of crisis team members tend to be vague or limited. The personal characteristics mentioned in the literature include being a team player, having decision-making ability, having listening skills, and being able to handle stress (Barton, 1993; Dilenschneider & Hyde, 1985; Littlejohn, 1983; Mitchell, 1986; Regester, 1989; Walsh, 1995). Unfortunately, little detail is provided about what actually constitutes these characteristics—the knowledge and skills needed to meet them. The following section is dedicated to providing detailed information about the tasks, knowledge, skills, and traits that make for an effective crisis team member. The task serves as the organizing point for the explanations.

Decision-Making Task

Crisis management is a group decision-making process (Fink, 1986; O'Connor, 1985; Williams & Olaniran, 1994). The three primary responsibilities of the crisis team all involve decision making. The CMT decides what goes into the CMP (Pauchant & Mitroff, 1992; Wilson & Patterson, 1987), when and how to enact the CMP (Mitroff, Harrington, & Gai, 1996; Walsh,

TABLE 5.1 Crisis Team Task Analysis

Task Statement	Knowledge	Skills	Traits
Work as a team to facilitate the achievement of crisis team goals	1. Understand various styles of conflict resolution 2. Understand components of a ethical conflict resolution	1. Ability to use cooperation-based conflict management style 2. Ability to apply components of ethical conflict resolution	1. Cooperative predisposition
Apply the crisis management plan (CMP) to crises to facilitate an effective organizational response to the crisis	1. Understand how to use the crisis management plan 2. Understand specialized information of one's functional area 3. Understand mechanisms for coping with stress 4. Understand mechanism for coping with ambiguity	1. Ability to follow directions given in the CMP 2. Ability to supply area-relevant information 3. Ability to the use the mechanisms for coping with stress 4. Ability to use the mechanisms for coping with ambiguity	1. Handle stress 2. Ambiguity tolerance
Make the group decisions necessary to solve effectively the problems encountered by the crisis team	1. Understand the critical vigilant decision-making functions 2. Understand the value of argumentation 3. Understand how to structure arguments 4. Understands the value of group participation	1. Ability to apply the elements of critical vigilant decision-making functions 2. Ability to create arguments 3. Ability to speak in groups	1. Argumentativeness 2. Willingness to speak in groups
Listen to others as a means of collecting information	1. Understand the steps to effective listening	1. Ability to use the steps to effective listening	

65

1995), and how to extemporaneously handle those factors not covered in the crisis plan. If crisis management is decision making, the knowledge, skills, and traits associated with group decision making should be essential to the effective performance of a crisis team.

Group decision-making research consistently has found vigilance to be valuable in making effective decisions and avoiding ineffective decisions (Hirokawa, 1985, 1988; Hirokawa & Rost, 1992). Vigilance is a form of critical thinking. Critical thinking can be defined as a structured process whereby people actively and carefully conceptualize, apply, analyze, synthesize, and evaluate the information they have collected from or created by observation, experience, reflection, reasoning, or communication as a guide to their actions or beliefs (Scriven & Paul, 1996, p. 1). Critical thinking involves learning skills used to evaluate information and applying those skills. Vigilance applies critical thinking to group decision making by emphasizing the need for careful and thorough analysis of all information related to a decision (Hirokawa & Rost, 1992; Williams & Olaniran, 1994). Analysis is a process of dissecting a whole into its parts to examine something in more detail.

Hirokawa and Rost (1992) identified a specific set of four critical vigilant decision-making functions that aid the decision-making process: problem analysis, standards for evaluating alternative choices, understanding the important positive aspects of an alternative choice, and understanding the important negative aspects of an alternative choice. Each of these skills is a corrective for a factor that could contribute to faulty decision making. First, a decision is threatened when a group fails to a see a problematic situation or identify the correct cause of the problematic situation. The group must analyze or assess the problem thoroughly and systematically. A group must understand what it is supposed to accomplish.

Second, a decision is threatened if the group improperly evaluates the alternative choices for solving a problem. Three critical vigilant decision-making functions address the evaluation of alternative choices. One, the group identifies appropriate standards for evaluating alternative choices; the group discusses and specifies criteria for evaluating alternative choices. Two, the group applies the criteria to understand the important positive aspects of an alternative choice; the group identifies and seeks clarification of the positive aspects of an alternative choice. And three, the group applies the criteria to understand the important negative aspects of an alternative choice; the group identifies and seeks clarification of the negative aspects of an alternative choice. Research in laboratories and in the field have found these four critical vigilance decision-making functions to be related to higher-quality decisions in groups (Hirokawa & Rost, 1992).

Vigilance is a composite of a variety of knowledge (K), skills (S), and traits (T). First, group members must know some process for evaluating situations (K) and be able to apply these processes (S) to their situations. Second, group members must know how to develop the criteria used to evaluate decision alternatives (K) and be able apply these criteria (S). And third, group members must be able to argue for thoroughness of analysis and to present their views on the matters being discussed (S). Arguing refers to giving reasons for and against a proposal, not fighting or an emotional disagreement (Paul & Elder, 1995). Group members must be motivated to use their skills if analysis is to be thorough (Hirokawa & Rost, 1992). This requires groups to continually argue for thoroughness. Group members must be willing to argue their positions (T) because group decisions become less effective when members do not voice concerns and allow one perspective to dominate the group's discussion (Hirokawa, 1985, 1988; Rancer, Baukus, & Infante, 1985). Group members are required to have the skills for argumentation and the disposition to argue (the argumenativeness trait). Table 5.1 provides the knowledge, skills, and traits associated with decision making.

Work as a Team Task

Members of the crisis team must be able to work together as a group. Team members must be able to function in a cooperative manner—to maximize the gains for themselves and others (Daniels, Spiker, & Papa, 1997). Some people are naturally cooperative, and others are competitive (Baron, 1983). Part of working together is resolving the conflict that occurs inevitably within groups (Kreps, 1990; O'Connor, 1985). Conflict happens when people are interdependent with one another but have conflicting goals that may prevent one another from reaching their goals (Putnam & Poole, 1987). People in groups disagree and can blame one another for the disagreements. Conflict can be beneficial to a group. Vigilance is fostered through conflict—arguing different perspectives. Cooperation is the key to conflict becoming productive rather than destructive (Kreps, 1990).

People seem to have preferred conflict styles—the typical mode a person uses to handle disputes (Putnam & Poole, 1987). There are systems for identifying conflict styles (Daniels et al., 1997; Kilmann & Thomas, 1975). The key is to emphasize the use of cooperation-based conflict styles in crisis team deliberations.

Enacting the CMP Task

The crisis team must be able to enact the CMP. For this reason, groups train by reviewing and practicing the CMP (Guth, 1993; Higbee, 1992; Loewendick, 1993; Regester, 1989; Wilsenbilt, 1989). Creating the CMP should give the team members greater understanding of the plan (Barton, 1993; Wilson & Patterson, 1987). This is where the team member's functional organizational area becomes important. One reason to appoint a team member is his or her particular knowledge of a functional area that is important during a crisis (e.g., legal, media relations, investor relations, etc.). The knowledge and skills of these functional areas are important to executing the crisis plan effectively. Stress enters the crisis management equation most fully during the execution of the plan (Dilenschneider & Hyde, 1985; Shrivastava & Mitroff, 1987). When the crisis team faces deadline pressures and needs to deal with ambiguous information, the stress it experiences increases (O'Connor, 1985). Table 5.1 identifies the knowledge, skills, and traits associated with enacting the crisis plan. Part of enacting the CMP is managing the concomitant stress and ambiguous information a crisis generates. Stress can hinder job performance (Baron, 1983), and ambiguity can create stress for people (Tsui, 1993).

Listening Task

Crisis team members use listening frequently. Collecting information when creating or enacting the CMP often means that CMT members must listen to others. Working together in a group to make decisions requires listening to other people in the group. Obviously, listening is an important part of many tasks. However, many crisis managers felt listening was important enough to be considered as a separate, distinct task.

Implications for Crisis Team Selection

Crisis team selection is not as simple as finding the people best qualified to work on the CMT. Selection is complicated by the need to have specific functional areas within the organization be represented on the CMT. The functional approach, the dominant selection criterion in the crisis management writings, argues that team members must represent specific functional divisions or positions within the organization. Typical positions included in the list are legal, security, public relations, operations/technical, safety, quality assurance, and representative of or the CEO (Barton, 1993; Pauchant

& Mitroff, 1992). The logic behind the functional selection is that certain knowledge bases (i.e., operations and legal), skills (i.e., media relations and public relations), and organizational power sources (i.e., CEO) are required on a crisis team. For instance, a crisis team often needs to integrate technical information about the organization's operations, assessment of legal concerns, and information collected by security when enacting a crisis plan. Furthermore, media relations skills are needed when addressing the press, and the CEO or his or her representative legitimizes the crisis team within the organization and empowers the team with the power to take action (Barton, 1993; Pauchant & Mitroff, 1992).

Team members must bring certain area-specific knowledge and skills to the crisis team that will facilitate the execution of the crisis plan. However, as Shrivastava and Mitroff (1987) noted, crisis team members should also have a set of general crisis management skills. The knowledge, skills, and traits featured in Table 5.1 represent a set of general crisis management skills that are vital to the effective operation of a crisis team. The full range of knowledge, skills, and traits should be considered when attempting to identify those people most likely to contribute positively to the crisis team. Assessment would aid in the screening of crisis team candidates. An organization may be in a position to choose among a number of people to represent a functional area. For instance, there might be a pool of five people from operations who possess the requisite skills and knowledge from their area. Only one person from operations is needed, and the organization wants the person best suited for work on a crisis team. The assessment instrument would indicate which of these potential candidates best matches the demands of being a crisis team member, particularly in terms of traits. Traits are highlighted because people can learn to cope with the limits of their traits but not to develop completely new traits.

It is possible to develop profiles of desirable and undesirable crisis team members from the traits in Table 5.1. A desirable crisis team member would be low in communication apprehension in groups, high in cooperation, high in ambiguity tolerance, moderate in argumentativeness, and well equipped to handle stress. The desirable profile produces a crisis team member who can work under stress, is not bothered by the ambiguity of a crisis, will work with the team to find the best solution, is willing to express opinions and ideas, and is willing to argue the merits and weaknesses of various solutions. An undesirable profile would be high in communication apprehension in groups, high in competitiveness, low in ambiguity tolerance, high in verbal aggressiveness, and poorly equipped to handle stress. The undesirable profile produces a team member who functions poorly under stress, feels increased stress in the ambiguous situations, works poorly in problem solving by fighting, and may be unwilling to contribute ideas and opinions.

Applications for Training

Crisis experts frequently mention the need to train crisis teams (Augustine, 1995; Loewendick, 1993; Mitroff et al., 1996; Pauchant & Mitroff, 1992; Walsh, 1995; Williams & Olaniran, 1994). In any job, a person must possess the necessary knowledge and skills if he or she is to perform effectively (Goldstein, 1993). Current training practices include group review of the CMP, crisis drills, simulation exercises, and outside consults providing training packages (Wilsenbilt, 1989). Discussions of crisis team training are dominated by practice based on running simulations of crises (Augustine, 1995; Birch, 1994; Mitchell, 1986; Pauchant & Mitroff, 1992; Regester, 1989; Walsh, 1995). There is sound logic to this application; simulations enable you to determine how well people can enact the CMP and how the CMP might be improved. Part of group training is determining that the team can accomplish group-level tasks (Goldstein, 1993). Crisis simulations emphasize group-level tasks with their focus on enacting the CMP. Although useful, the group-level approach to training overlooks the need to train the individual-level skills needed to complete crisis team tasks. People need individual-level knowledge and skills to function as effective team members (Stohl & Coombs, 1988). Williams and Olaniran (1994) noted that crisis team members must be trained in specific crisis duties. Specific crisis duties include the individual-level knowledge and skills needed to be effective team members.

The individual-level assessment would be composed of the knowledge, skills, and traits listed in Table 5.1. The individual-level assessment of each team member indicates specific areas where a person is strong or weak. The individual-level analyses identify a person's specific training needs. Training should be specific—people should be trained only in those areas in which they are deficient. A crisis team assessment system not only determines a person's strengths and weaknesses but also evaluates a person's progress in acquiring knowledge and skills (Goldstein, 1993). The initial assessment is the benchmark or baseline against which subsequent assessments are compared. Specific training modules would be developed for the major knowledge and skills important to a crisis team. When needed, modules designed to help people cope with the limits of specific traits could be added. An illustration would be a module designed to develop listening skills.

Crisis teams need training. A 1992 Public Relations Society of America study found that only 63% of U.S. companies with CMPs have engaged in any type of crisis training in the past 2 years (Guth, 1993). This suggests that even organizations that have CMPs and CMTs are not truly prepared to face a crisis. Crisis team training should require the consideration of both individual-level and group-level knowledge and skills. Part of evaluating crisis simulations would be dedicated to examining individual-level skills, a point that is missing in most current discussions of crisis team training.

The Spokesperson

The spokesperson is the voice of the organization during the crisis. As such, the spokesperson is a very important and specialized function within the CMT. A poorly trained or unskilled spokesperson merely exacerbates the crisis situation (Donath, 1984; Mitchell, 1986). Again, selection and training require the identification of tasks and the knowledge, skills, and traits associated with those tasks. The discussion of the spokesperson begins with an analysis of the spokesperson's role—his or her responsibilities during a crisis. The spokesperson's role provides a foundation for locating the requisite knowledge, skills, and traits.

The Spokesperson's Role

Saying that the spokesperson is the voice of the organization during a crisis is a simplification of the role. The primary responsibility of the spokesperson is to manage the accuracy and consistency of the messages coming from the organization (Carney & Jorden, 1993; Seitel, 1983). Message management is not an easy task and usually involves more than one person. Every organization should have multiple spokespersons. Although multiple spokespersons may seem to contradict the view that the organization speak with one voice, really it does not. First, one person cannot be relied on all the time. What if that person is unavailable during a crisis? That individual might be on a vacation thousands of miles away and cannot reach the crisis center in time. What if the crisis drags on for days, requiring 24-hours-a-day efforts from the CMT? No one person can perform his or her job effectively for 24 to 48 hours straight. Eventually, lack of sleep will take its toll on job performance. Therefore, each organization should a have pool of spokespersons all selected and trained in advance of a crisis (Fearn-Banks, 1996).

Second, it is an overstatement to equate the idea of one voice with one person. An organization speaking with one voice merely implies that the organization presents a consistent message. Working together, multiple spokespersons can share one voice. However, the teamwork so vital to the CMT becomes a premium here. The media want to question authoritative sources during a crisis. No one person in an organization is an authority on every subject. As a result, an organization may have a number of people available during one press conference. Each question is then answered by the person most qualified to address the question (Lerbinger, 1997). The key is preparation of all spokespersons, including the sharing of all relevant information, and the coordination of the questions and spokespersons.

Clearly the spokesperson must be able to work with the media. Working with the media involves listening and responding to questions. Listening is essential because a spokesperson cannot give an appropriate answer to a question if he or she does not hear the question correctly (Stewart & Cash, 1997). Answering questions demands the ability to think quickly. Press conferences are not slow-moving events. The spokesperson must be able to answer questions rapidly. Compounding all of this is the fact that the spokesperson is doing his or her job in a time of high stress—the organization is in crisis, and the media want answers immediately. A spokesperson must be able to handle stress well and cannot let stress interfere with handling media inquires. The spokesperson is a member of the crisis team, so all the knowledge, skills, and traits in Table 5.1 still apply. However, the big difference between spokespersons and other crisis team members stems from the need to work with the media.

Crisis experts continually recommend that the spokesperson have media training. Media training usually means practice with responding to media questions—the spokesperson has gone through rehearsals (Fearn-Banks, 1996; Nicholas, 1995; Sonnenfeld, 1994). Furthermore, there are a variety of laundry lists for what spokespersons should and should not do (e.g., Katz, 1987; Lukaszewski, 1987; Pines, 1985). A sample list of spokesperson "dos and don'ts" include the following: be truthful, never say "no comment," be concise and clear, do not lose your temper or argue with journalists, correct errors and misinformation in questions that are asked, look pleasant on camera, and appear in control and concerned. Although such lists are of some help, they fail to provide a systematic means of either selecting or training a spokesperson.

Media-Specific Tasks of the Spokesperson

From watching television, we all recognize that some people are well suited to media appearances and others are not. Some people look good on television, and others look like criminals (Nicholas, 1995). Oddly, one task of the spokesperson is to be appealing to the viewers. This does not mean the spokesperson must be physically attractive. Rather, he or she must present material in an attractive fashion. Media training is often vague in explaining how to present material in an attractive fashion. Similar to the section on CMTs, Table 5.2 summarizes the primary tasks of the spokesperson along with the salient knowledge, skills, and traits necessary to perform tasks.

A mix of content and delivery concerns confronts any spokesperson giving a public presentation. Content concerns emphasize the information being presented. The spokesperson must disseminate accurate information about the crisis situation (Mitchell, 1986; Trahan, 1993). A spokesperson must have command over the crisis-related information if he or she is to convey this information to the media and other stakeholders. However, poor delivery skills can prevent a message from being received accurately (Holladay & Coombs, 1994; McCroskey, 1997). A spokesperson must be skilled at presenting messages to the target stakeholders—in this case, the media. Each of the four spokesperson tasks will be explained along with an analysis of the task's connection to content and delivery.

Pleasant on Camera

Appearing pleasant on camera is not a superficial observation that the spokesperson should look good. Instead, being pleasant on camera reflects a set of delivery skills that helps the spokesperson achieve a number of important crisis objectives. Previously it was noted that the CMT must show concern and control during a crisis. Part of the perception of concern and control is developed through the way the spokesperson presents the crisis-related information. One way to better understand delivery is to consider it as part of communicator style. Communicator style is the way in which a person communicates; it reflects the way in which something is communicated and not just the content of the message (Norton, 1983). Communicator style influences how the content of the message is interpreted. Style provides a frame for how people should view the content of a message (Holladay & Coombs, 1994).

TABLE 5.2 Spokesperson Media Task Analysis

Task Statement	Knowledge	Skills
Appear pleasant on camera	1. Understand the value of proper delivery	1. Strong delivery
Answer questions effectively	1. Understand danger of long pauses 2. Understand the steps to effective listening 3. Appreciate the danger of "no comment" 4. Understand the danger of arguing with reporters	1. Able to think quickly 2. Able to use the steps to effective listening 3. Able to use phrases other than "no comment" when an answer is not currently known 4. Able to stay calm under pressure
Present crisis information clearly	1. Appreciate the problems with jargon 2. Understands the need to structure responses	1. Able to avoid the use of jargon 2. Able to organize responses
Can handle difficult questions	1. Understands the characteristics of tough questions	1. Able to identify tough questions 2. Able to ask for questions to be reworded 3. Able to preface tough questions in a tactful manner 4. Able to challenge incorrect information in a question 5. Able to explain why an answer cannot be answered 6. Able to evaluate the appropriateness of multiple-choice responses in a question 7. Able to respond to questions with multiple parts

Spokespersons would want to maximize the style elements that cultivate the perceptions of control and compassion. Compassion is developed through the attentive and friendly style elements. Attentive styles reflect empathy and listening by the spokesperson. Being friendly suggests a person is confirming and giving positive recognition to others (Norton, 1983). The attentive and friendly style elements will help to cultivate the perception that the spokesperson is compassionate because compassionate people are empathetic and confirming. The dominant style elements mean a person is behaving in a confident and businesslike manner (Norton, 1983). The dominant style facilitates the perception that the spokesperson is in control of the situation.

Maximizing these three style elements requires attention to specific delivery factors. The spokespersons must learn to maintain consistent eye contact with the audience (i.e., looking at the audience at least 60% of the time), should use hand gestures to emphasize points, should vary their voices to avoid being monotone, should be sure to change facial expressions to avoid being blank faced, and should avoid too many verbal disfluencies such as "uhs," "erhs," and "uhms." Spokespersons should be trained to maximize these five delivery variables when they present material to the media and other stakeholders. Past research indicates that the five delivery factors promote the perception of dominance, attentiveness, and friendliness as well as make a person more credible (Burgoon, Birk, & Pfau, 1990; Holladay & Coombs, 1994). In turn, the spokesperson will be perceived to be compassionate and in control of the crisis situation. It is logical to conclude that the spokesperson will be perceived more positively by stakeholders when maximizing these five delivery factors.

There is a flip side to delivery as well—poor delivery leads to negative perceptions of the spokesperson. Poor delivery skills are often interpreted as signs of deception (de Turck & Miller, 1985; Feeley & de Turck, 1995). People doubt the believability of a message when these delivery factors are present: (a) have weak eye contact and look at people infrequently; (b) have frequent disfluencies (i.e., "uhs," "ums," etc.); (c) use adaptors, abnormal hand or arm movements associated with fidgeting; and (d) spend too much time using hand gestures (de Turck & Miller, 1985; Feeley & de Turck, 1995). Basically, we all have clues we look for when trying to detect deception. Part of the clues we look for are the four delivery factors just reviewed.

Delivery has always been an important part of the presentation of a public message (Heinberg, 1963; McCroskey, 1997). Content can never be forgotten because good delivery does not make up for lack of content. Rather, good delivery enhances the reception of a message, but poor delivery detracts from the reception of a message. Spokespersons should be trained to maximize the delivery factors that promote control and compassion while minimizing those that contribute to perceptions of deception. All of the delivery factors covered in this chapter can be taught. However, it helps if people do not exhibit the communication apprehension trait when speaking in public. Although communication apprehension can be overcome, you start at a higher delivery proficiency level when you have spokespersons who are not communication apprehensive (McCroskey, 1970, 1972). Part of the spokesperson's media training should include efforts to make people aware of their delivery habits and to polish their delivery skills.

Answer Questions Effectively

Answering questions effectively means providing responses to the questions that are asked. Preparation is essential to effective answers. The spokesperson must know or be able to retrieve quickly the crisis information that has been collected to that point. Another part is listening to hear the question. Spokespersons should not answer the questions they wanted to be asked; they must hear and respond to the questions asked by the reporters. Sometimes the spokesperson does not know the answer. The correct response is to admit what you do not know but promise to deliver the information as soon as you get it (Stewart & Cash, 1997). Remember the rule to never say "no comment." The "no comment" triggers two negative events. First, 65% of stakeholders who hear or see the "no comment" equate it with the organization saying it is guilty ("In a Crisis," 1993). Second, "no comment" is a form of silence. Silence is a very passive response (Brummett, 1980). In a crisis, being passive means that other actors in the crisis event get to speak and interpret the crisis event for your stakeholders (Hearit, 1994). The organization is allowing others who may be ill informed, may be misinformed, or hold a grudge against the organization to define the crisis for stakeholders. An interpretation based on the wrong information or information supplied by an enemy can only hurt the organization's reputation.

The spokesperson also must be cordial and not argue with reporters (Mackinnon, 1996; Nicholas, 1995). Being cordial brings us back to the personality traits of a good crisis team member. A spokesperson should not be high in verbal aggressiveness or argumentativeness. Either traits can lead to an argument with reporters. This does not mean that a spokesperson lets incorrect statements stand. Instead, the spokesperson corrects any errors or misinformation before answering a question but should not debate the error or misinformation (Mackinnon, 1996). Handling stress is a part of answering questions too. An inability to handle stress should reduce a spokesperson's ability to answer questions effectively because too much stress reduces task performance in general. Stress is high during media encounters due to the time pressure and the need to answer multiple questions from a variety of reporters (Balik, 1995).

Present Crisis Information Clearly

Presenting information clearly focuses on the content of the response. As such, it is related to answering questions effectively but has a narrower focus. The focus is on the stakeholders being able to understand what the spokesperson said. The spokesperson's answers must be clear and concise. Clear means the answer is free of organizational jargon and overly technical terms and details (Mackinnon, 1996). Jargon is meaningless to those outside of the circle using it (Nicholas, 1995). As a result, jargon only clouds an answer. Overly technical information produces the same hazy reception of the message. In addition, technobabble makes people think that the organization is using jargon to avoid telling the truth. Use only the necessary technical information and explain it in such a way that nontechnical people can understand it. PepsiCo's handling of its 1993 syringe scare exemplifies how to translate technical information. In June 1993, reports began to surface that syringes were being found in cans of Diet Pespi. PepsiCo chose to focus on how it would be virtually impossible for a syringe to get into the can during bottling. PepsiCo reduced its bottling process to easily understandable terms for the news media and its consumers. PepsiCo believed and later proved the syringe scare was a hoax (Magiera, 1993; Mohr, 1994; Weinstein, 1993; Zinn & Regan, 1993). Clarity is aided by careful organization of the response (Stewart & Cash, 1997). An organized answer is easier to understand than a rambling answer.

Handle Difficult Questions

During a press conference, not all questions are of equal caliber. Watch any press conference on television and you will see exceedingly long and complicated questions, questions that are multiple questions (ask for several pieces of information), tricky and tough questions, questions that are based on erroneous information, and multiple-choice questions with unacceptable choice options. These five examples represent the difficult questions faced by a spokesperson. The spokesperson must learn to recognize difficult questions and respond appropriately. Recognition involves practicing listening to questions delivered in the press conference format. Each of the five tough questions have identifiable features.

Recognition is easier than providing the response to a tough question. Still, there are response strategies for each of the five tough questions. For long, complicated questions, ask for the question to be repeated, rephrased, or explained. These strategies give the media representative a chance to improve the question's wording and clarity while providing the spokesperson with more time to construct a response. Multiple questions in one question can be handled in one of two ways. First, the spokesperson can choose which part of the question he or she will respond to. The spokesperson should select the part of the question that fits best with providing the organization's desired message. Second, a spokesperson can address all parts of the question. When responding to all or multiple parts of a question, the spokesperson should number each part and the answer to each part. The additional structure helps to clarify the answer for other audience members.

Questions that are tricky or tough need a tactful preface to the answer. The spokesperson must convey to the audience that the question is tough or tricky and that a longer than usual answer is needed to address the question. It may also be the case that the tricky or tough question cannot be answered, and the spokesperson must explain why the question cannot be answered (Stewart & Cash, 1997). A question based on erroneous information must be challenged and corrected (Nicholas, 1995). The spokesperson must make sure that misinformation is removed from the crisis information being presented at the press conference. For multiple-choice questions, the spokesperson must determine if the response options are fair (Stewart & Cash, 1997). Why should a spokesperson choose a response when the two options might be having the organization categorized as being heartless or stupid? The spokesperson should explain that the options are unreasonable or inappropriate and develop his or her own option that fits with the question. Training helps a spokesperson identify and develop effective responses to the tough questions.

The Crisis Management Plan

The core sermon preached by crisis converts is the need for a detailed but usable CMP. The CMP must contain the information needed to manage a crisis but should not be too long and cumbersome. Long CMPs look nice on shelves as they collect dust but are not practical when a crisis hits (Barton, 1993, 1995). This section reviews the value of a CMP and details the basics that should be included in it.

Value of the CMP

Crises are time-pressured events in which quick responses are essential. A CMP helps to reduce response time by precollecting needed background information, preidentifying responsibilities, and assigning certain actions to specific individuals that must be taken when a crisis hits. During a crisis, time should not be wasted finding the background information, deciding who will do what, and trying to determine the sequence of events (Barton, 1993). In addition to speed, the CMP creates an organized and efficient response. A CMP creates a system that can save lives, reduce an organization's exposure to risks, and permit remedial actions to be taken without embarrassment and scrutiny (Barton, 1995).

Many large organizations have recognized the need for a CMP (Barton, 1993; Lerbinger, 1997). Still, only 56.9% of major companies, up from 53% in 1984, have CMPs. The numbers indicate that the message is still not being heard by all organizations (Guth, 1995). Sometimes it takes a crisis to reinforce the need for a CMP. Of companies with CMPs, 13% developed them after experiencing a crisis (Barton, 1993). The phrase "better late then never" comes to mind. In reality, all organizations should have CMPs because all organizations are at risk of a crisis no matter how careful they are about their policies and operations.

Components of a CMP

The CMP is, at its roots, a communication document. The CMP involves identifying who to contact and how. It also includes means for documenting what was said or not said during a crisis. In fact, some crisis experts refer to the CMP as the crisis communication plan (i.e., Barry, 1984; Fearn-Banks, 1996). However, the more precise terminology is the crisis management plan. A crisis communication plan is a major part of the larger CMP. This section identifies the main sections typically comprising a CMP, explains what goes into each section, and notes the function of each section.

1. *Cover page.* The cover page identifies the document as the CMP, notes the document is confidential, provides the revision date, and records the

number of copies. Confidentiality reminds employees that the CMP should not be copied or shown to people outside of the organization, and the numbering is used to control the number of copies in circulation. The revision date allows for a quick check to determine how up-to-date the CMP is.

2. *Introduction.* The introduction is a message typically written by the CEO. The introduction is used to highlight the importance of the CMP and persuade employees to take it seriously (Barton, 1993; Fearn-Banks, 1996).

3. *Acknowledgments.* The acknowledgments is a removable page that employees sign and return to human resources where it is placed in their personnel files. It is a form of signed affidavit saying that the employee has read and understands the CMP. Having a signed document in one's personnel file encourages the employee to take the CMP very seriously (Barton, 1993).

4. *Rehearsal dates.* The rehearsal dates record when the plan has been practiced. The rehearsal date is another check on how up-to-date the plan and the crisis team are (Fearn-Banks, 1996).

5. *Crisis management team.* The CMT section lists the incident commander for the team, how to reach the incident commander, how to activate the CMP (who should place the calls), and when the CMP should be activated (when a situation is defined as a crisis). The crisis team section is the means of starting the crisis management process.

6. *CMT contact sheet.* The contact sheet lists the names of all the members of the team, their areas of expertise, any outside consultants that may be needed, any outside agents that should be contacted such as insurance or emergency personnel, and complete contact information for how to reach each team member, consultant, and outside agent. The CMT contact sheet section indicates who to contact, tells why they are relevant to a crisis, and provides a variety of means for contacting each person. This document is sometimes called the crisis directory. The CMT contact sheet provides an easy-to-use system for identifying and reaching members of the crisis team (Barton, 1993; Fearn-Banks, 1996).

7. *Crisis risk assessment.* Every organization should anticipate what crises it may face. The crisis risk assessment identifies possible crises and evaluates the risk of each crisis in terms of probability and impact. Prob-

ability is the likelihood of the crisis occurring, and impact is the amount of damage (financial, structural, environmental, reputational, or human) the crisis could inflict on the organization. The assessment exercise is part of an organization's effort to show that it engaged in due diligence. The crisis risk assessment works hand-in-hand with the crisis portfolio. The crisis risk assessment is not as detailed as the crisis portfolio. The crisis risk assessment merely overviews the variety of crises an organization may face and is not an exhaustive analysis of all possible crises (Barton, 1993). The crisis assessment was detailed at the beginning of this chapter.

8. *Incident report.* Crisis teams must keep accurate records of what was done during a crisis. The incident report sheets are tools used to record this vital documentation. Crisis teams need this information when evaluating their crisis management efforts, and the organization needs this information when handling lawsuits or government investigations triggered by the crisis. The documentation centers on identifying when the incident was first discovered, where the crisis occurred, and when various people and organizations were contacted about the crisis (Barton, 1993; Fearn-Banks, 1996).

9. *Proprietary information.* Although crisis managers preach full disclosure of information, there are some policies and factual information an organization cannot reveal. The proprietary information section reminds managers that certain information is confidential and cannot be released to stakeholders without CEO authorization or review by legal council (Tyler, 1997). For example, an organization should never give away its trade secrets that provide its competitive edge in the marketplace without an extremely compelling reason (Barton, 1993). On a related note, an organization should never release the names of victims until family members have been notified.

10. *CMT strategy worksheet.* Crisis managers must remember that communication is strategic—it serves a distinct purpose. The CMT worksheet reminds CMT members of what it means to be strategic and document crisis actions. Crisis managers are prompted to consider who they are talking to (the exact stakeholder), record the specific audience, consider what they are trying to achieve with this communication (goals), record the specific goal, and attach a copy of the actual message that was sent to the audience (Barton, 1993). Crisis managers can add other pertinent message construction reminders that are specific to their organization. For example, reminders about the use of specific technical terms can be added. A sample technical term reminder might describe the difference between

"venting" and "releasing." Each organization should develop its own set of additional reminders.

11. *Secondary contact sheet.* Stakeholders other than those listed on the CMT contact sheet may need to be contacted during a crisis. These stakeholders may have information the organization needs or may need to be notified about the crisis. The secondary contact sheet identifies the stakeholders to be contacted and who in the organization is responsible for communicating with this stakeholder. The type of stakeholder, name of the contact person(s) for that stakeholder group, their organizational affiliation (if applicable), their title, contact information, and documentation for the contact (when was contact made and by whom) should be included on the sheet (Barton, 1993). The secondary contact sheet is an extension of the stakeholder communication network. An organization that maps its stakeholder communication network will already have all the information necessary to compile the outside agent section of the CMT contact sheet and the entire secondary contact sheet.

12. *Stakeholder contact worksheet.* During a crisis, various stakeholders will be contacting the organization. Foremost among those are the media. The stakeholder contact worksheet should begin with the specific procedures that should be used when a call is received (Barton, 1993). The procedures should specify where all calls should be routed and who will answer the calls. The focus typically is on identifying a spokesperson to respond to the media, a topic discussed earlier in the chapter. However, the organization should not overlook other stakeholders who may be seeking information such as community leaders, employees, employees' families, or investors. Although a lower priority than the media during a crisis, these other stakeholders have legitimate information needs. Neglecting these stakeholders injures the organization-stakeholder relationship. Organizations must develop procedures for all stakeholders that might contact the organization, not just the media. In addition to procedures, careful documentation is essential. To record this information, multiple copies of a stakeholder contact worksheet should be included in the CMP. The stakeholder contact includes who contacted the organization, when the contact was made, the channel used to contact the organization, the specific inquiry, the response, and any follow-up that was promised.

13. *Business resumption plan.* One organizational goal during a crisis is to resume "business as usual" as soon as possible. The business resumption plan details what an organization will do if the crisis damages the facility or vital equipment needed to conduct business. Although it may be

a separate document, the CMP must acknowledge and recommend the use of the business resumption plan when necessary (Barton, 1995).

14. *Crisis control center.* When the CMP is activated, team members need to know where they should assemble. Some progressive organizations have developed special crisis control centers, sometimes called crisis command centers. Team members know to go directly to the crisis control center when they are contacted (Barton, 1993; Fearn-Banks, 1996).

15. *Postcrisis evaluation.* Once a crisis is over, the CMT must assess its efforts. As Chapter 8 will detail, an organization must learn from its crises. Because the crisis management effort is primarily an exercise in communication—information collection and dissemination—the evaluation form focuses on communication (Barton, 1993; Egelhoff & Sen, 1992; Fearn-Banks, 1996). The evaluation contains sections on the notification system used by the CMT and on the information collection efforts of the CMT. The information collected by the form will help the CMT to correct weaknesses and maintain strengths of the CMP.

CMP Is Not Enough

The danger of a CMP is that it can provide managers with a false sense of security. Some managers feel that if they have a CMP, they are protected when a crisis hits. Three flaws challenge this assumption. First, the CMP is a general guideline for action—the CMPs represent contingencies. Crisis teams must adapt the CMP to match the precise crisis. Mindlessly following a CMP in lockstep fashion is a recipe for disaster (Fink, 1986; Littlejohn, 1983). The CMT is valuable in adapting the CMP to contingencies and handling those factors never addressed in the CMT (Barton, 1993; Register, 1989).

Second, the CMP is a living document. Organizations change, and their operating environments change, as well as their personnel; thus, the CMP must be updated regularly. At least once or twice a year the CMP should be examined for necessary changes. Third, a CMP has little value if it is not practiced in simulations. Practice reveals the holes or weaknesses that must be addressed before a real crisis occurs (Wilsenbilt, 1989). For example, at an airport in Texas, a serious flaw was discovered during the crisis drill for an airplane crash. Because airport personnel had the wrong frequency for emergency personnel in the town, their radios were worthless during the drill. Changing the frequencies was a simple procedure, but the problem would not have been discovered without the drill. The drill rather than an actual crisis revealed serious problems in the CMP. Furthermore, practice is the only way for team members to gain experience enacting the plan, one of their primary tasks. The dangers of unrehearsed teams has already been addressed. Managers must not let the CMP lull them into a false sense of security. An ongoing approach to crisis management should prevent this complacency.

APPLICATION POINT

Critiquing a CMP will help you to understand how to write a more thorough CMP. Find a copy of a CMP. Compare that CMP to the points covered in this chapter. Where is the CMP lacking? Why might the CMP have not used certain points covered in this chapter? What would you do to improve the CMP? Explain how each of your corrective actions would improve the CMP.

Preparation of the Crisis Communication System

With the personnel and CMP in place, crisis managers must make sure the physical setup of the communication system is prepared. Preparation entails determining if the crisis communication system is sufficient to meet the needs of the CMT and to verify that the system is operational—it works.

Crisis Control Center

The review of the CMP noted that organizations should have a crisis control center. The crisis control center serves many functions: It is a place for the CMT to meet and discuss the crisis, an information collection center, and a place for briefing the media. Ideally, the crisis control center is a separate area in the organization devoted solely to crisis management and equipped to meet the needs of the CMT. Large, geographically dispersed organizations should have crisis control centers at all major facilities. Multiple crisis control centers provide two benefits. First, a global company cannot expect to handle all crises effectively from one location. Extreme distances and time differences will hamper the crisis management effort. Second, multiple crisis control centers provide natural backups. If a crisis, such as a fire or earthquake, were to destroy an entire facility, the organization could use one of its other crisis control centers. Some smaller organizations may use a public relations agency to counsel their crisis response and use the agency's facilities for the crisis control center.

To fulfill its various functions, a crisis control center will have a scenario planing room for the CMT members to meet, a communication center for monitoring information (TV monitors, phones, computers, and wire service), and a press room for briefings. The crisis control center must be fully equipped and operational. Part of being prepared is having backups for all the necessary equipment. The specific equipment will vary according to the needs of the specific organization. Barton (1993) and Fearn-Banks (1996) both provide extensive lists of the equipment needed for a crisis control center. There must be sufficient equipment and backups for the center. The equipment must be checked regularly to ensure that it is in working order.

APPLICATION POINT

Develop an extensive list of equipment you would include in a crisis control center. As part of the list, briefly explain the relevance of each item to the crisis management process.

The Intranet and Internet

Intranets are relatively new technology but are custom-made for crises. Intranets are like the Internet but are self-contained within an organization. Self-contained means that only organizational members have access to the information, and even then access to sensitive information is limited to only those with the proper clearance (Hibbard, 1997). The beauty of the intranet is the speed of accessing information. The CMT can access information directly with key strokes on a computer instead of through telephone calls. If the crisis team needs financial information, it can retrieve the information on the computer—no need to place a call. Information processing is crucial during a crisis. Crisis teams do gather raw data, transform the data into usable information (interpreting the data), store the information, and communicate the information to others (Egelhoff & Sen, 1992). The intranet is ideal for meeting these needs (National Research Council, 1996; Reeves, 1996). Motorola, for example, uses an intranet as part of its crisis management efforts. Motorola stores crisis-relevant information on its intranet (e.g., financial and product information) and uses the system to facilitate the exchange of information during a crisis.

The intranet allows immediate access to data about the organization, is a place to store information, can provide a site where the crisis situation and relevant information are updated regularly and can be accessed by any employee, and allows communication to others in the organization via e-mail. Granted, not all crisis-relevant information can be collected via the intranet. For instance, interviewing witnesses to an accident in a facility must be done in person. However, any precrisis background data needed about the organization, such as product ingredients or safety records, can be located there. Moreover, e-mail and an intranet are not always appropriate means of communicating crisis-related information to employees. Still, employee e-mail can be effective at times, and a regularly updated summary of the crisis allows employees to access the type of crisis information they want when they want it.

The Internet provides access to information outside of the organization. Some forms of external information required during a crisis can be drawn from the Internet. In particular, government agencies provide information on regulations and reporting procedures. Other sources might be relevant depending on the type of crisis being experienced. For instance, industry accident data are useful during an organization's own accident crisis.

The Internet also allows outside stakeholders to access organizational information. Outside stakeholders can use e-mail or visit a Web page to access organizational information. In situations when it is an appropriate channel, e-mail can be used to reach government officials, media representatives, activist groups, stockholders, and many other stakeholders. The only limit is whether your target stakeholders have e-mail. A Web page can post updated information about the crisis. Again, stakeholders have the option of deciding what information they examine and when they examine it. Odwalla developed a Web page when it needed to recall some of its fruit drinks in 1996. The voluntary recall and consumer communications were launched because of reports that people were becoming ill from *E. coli* in Odwalla fruit drinks ("Nearly 200," 1996). The Web site identified the exact products under recall, how to return these products, and the reasons for the recall—the exact information customers needed to receive. Sample Odwalla messages included Odwalla's completion of the recall (November 2), an update on the recall (November 1), confirmation that the FDA found *E. coli* (November 4), and Odwalla expressing condolences to the Denver family whose child died from *E. coli* poisoning (November 8). The intranet and

Internet can be valuable information-processing and delivery tools when used properly during a crisis. Remember, the intranet and Internet do not make all other information-gathering and dissemination tools and channels obsolete. Always use the channel that is most effective for the communication situation (Clampitt, 1991; Rupp, 1996).

Conclusion

The preparation phase of crisis management anticipates the occurrence of crises. The organization musters the resources necessary to effectively manage the crises that may befall it. The central resources to muster are a diagnosis of vulnerabilities, a review of crisis types, selection and training of the crisis team, selection and training of the spokesperson(s), development of the CMP, and review of the crisis communication system. Diagnosing vulnerabilities assesses the likelihood and impact of potential organizational crises. Crisis types are groupings of similar crises. An organization cannot prepare for all crises but can prepare for the major crisis types. The diagnosis of vulnerabilities and the information about crisis types are used to construct the crisis portfolio, the individual crisis plans for each of the major crisis types.

The crisis team is responsible for managing the actual crisis. Therefore, it is essential to carefully select and fully train each crisis team member. The spokesperson is a specialized role within the crisis management process. This vital link to stakeholders must also be carefully selected and thoroughly trained. Failure to select and train crisis team members and spokespersons methodically is a recipe for disastrous crisis management. A crisis team is lost without a CMP. The CMP should be meticulously crafted before a crisis occurs. The various elements of a useful CMP were reviewed. Finally, the crisis communication system must be in working order. The CMP will prescribe how and when to communicate during a crisis. An excellent CMP and CMT are useless if the physical structure of the communication system is not in proper working order. Calls cannot be made without working phones, and online data cannot be accessed without working computer stations. All six of the preparation elements should be reviewed and updated regularly to maintain a state of readiness for crises. When crises begin to emerge, crisis management moves to the crisis recognition phase, the subject of Chapter 6.

6

Crisis Recognition

The actual crisis puts an organization's crisis preparation to the test. We deceive ourselves into believing that crises are easy to spot. We think all crises are like giant icebergs in the North Atlantic on a clear summer's day, relatively simple to see and avoid. Crises are easy to locate when there is an obvious trigger event: a train derails, a natural gas pipeline explodes, *E. coli* is found in frozen lasagna, a worker is wounded by a coworker, or some other identifiable event occurs. The obvious crises make it easy to realize the need to implement the crisis management plan (CMP). However, not all crises are obvious.

Crises are symbolic as well as objective. People can disagree whether a situation is a crisis. Some, particularly those involving conflicts with outside groups, are hard to see. As strange as this may sound, an organization may not even know it is in a crisis (Kamer, 1996). A situation becomes a crisis when key stakeholders agree it is a crisis. Unfortunately, some members of management may wish to deny that the organization is in a crisis even when stakeholders are screaming that it exists (Fink, Beak, & Taddeo, 1971; Pauchant & Mitroff, 1992). Similarly, management may refuse to take preventative actions—address prodromes. The first part of this chapter details how crisis team members might "sell" a crisis to top management in an organization. The recommendations hold true for selling prodromes too.

The crisis team begins to understand the crisis once it has uncovered one. The team members need to collect data, convert the raw data into usable information, store the information, and relay the necessary information to internal and, perhaps, to external organizational stakeholders—especially expert and governmental organizations. The crisis team must collect accurate crisis data quickly (Darling, 1994; Mitchell, 1986). The crisis team analyzes the data (processes the data) to create the crisis-related information that is used to guide decision making and create the messages sent to the various stakeholders. Without crisis-related information, the crisis team cannot make decisions or take actions to ameliorate the effects of the crisis. Actions include making statements to the media, the stakeholder most likely to be pressuring the organization for crisis information. Crisis management team (CMT) members must be aware of the problems associated with data collection and information processing. The second part of this chapter reviews research concerning the pitfalls associated with information collection, processing, and dissemination along with ideas for combating these problems.

Selling the Crisis

Although more the exception than the rule, some crises are not obvious or easily accepted. A problem can be ignored or not deemed worthy of the label *crisis* (Billings, Milburn, & Schaalman, 1980). Whether or not a problem is defined as a crisis is significant. Framing a problem as a crisis changes how the organization responds to it. When a problem becomes defined as a crisis, the organization expends more resources on the problem and works harder to discover an explanation for it (Dutton, 1986). Part of expending resources includes activation of the CMP. Although some crises may be hard to see, others are simply ignored. Stakeholder perception matters during a crisis (Augustine, 1995; Frank, 1994; Higbee, 1992). If your customers define a situation as a crisis, it is a crisis even if the dominant coalition chooses to initially define it as a noncrisis. We have to go no further than the Intel pentium chip flaw fiasco to experience the wisdom of these words. Intel knew in the summer of 1994 that the chip was flawed—could make mistakes on certain advanced mathematical calculations. However, Intel ignored customer concerns about the chip flaw. Intel even failed to grasp the significance of having the flaw posted on the Internet. After generating greater customer animosity, Intel eventually agreed the situation was a crisis and replaced the defective chip in December 1994 (Gonzalez-Herrero & Pratt, 1996). It may fall to the crisis team to convince the dominant coalition to accept the stakeholder perception that a crisis exists. A crisis is taken more seriously and is given more attention than a noncrisis. The issue for crisis managers becomes how to sell a problem as a crisis to the dominant coalition.

Crisis Framing: A Symbolic Response to Crises

All problems within organizations are framed in some way. A frame is the way a problem is presented, the meaning one attaches to the problem (Fairhurst & Sarr, 1996). A frame affects interpretations of the problem by highlighting certain of its features while masking other features (Dutton & Ashford, 1993). There can be competing frames. For example, abortion has been framed as both freedom of choice and murder. Organizational environments are filled with ambiguous events. Organizational members frequently decide if something is important or try to determine why something happened (Fairhurst & Sarr, 1996). Crises are part of the ambiguity encountered by organizations. Crisis managers need to create a frame that will provoke the most desirable response from top management. Three factors play a role in developing an appealing crisis frame: the crisis dimensions, the expertise of the dominant coalition, and the persuasiveness of the presentation.

Crisis Dimensions

Crises vary along three dimensions: perceived importance, immediacy, and uncertainty. Like prodromes, actual crises differ in the amount of loss that can occur and the likelihood of the loss if the CMP is not enacted. Failure to act can allow damage to spread to other areas of an organization, into surrounding communities, or to additional stakeholders. Fire or toxic gas can spread to other parts of a facility or into the community. Shareholders can suffer when financial damage from a product defect is not contained. Perceived importance is related to the crisis assessment dimensions of impact and likelihood. The perceived importance of a crisis varies with the value of the possible loss (impact) and the probability of the loss (likelihood). The greater the possible loss or probability of loss, the greater the perceived importance of a crisis (Billings et al., 1980; Dutton, 1986). For instance, a faulty product that affects a few customers has less perceived importance than a faulty product used by hundreds of thousands of customers if the potential harms from the defects are equal. Perceived importance is the key to framing prodromes. Crisis managers use likelihood and impact to rate prodromes (refer to Chapter 3). Similarly, crisis managers need to emphasize the danger of ignoring prodromes when presenting them to the dominant coalition.

Immediacy is the time pressure involved with the crisis. Time pressure has two components: how quickly the crisis will hit and the amount of stakeholder pressure to take action. The sooner a crisis can produce harm, the greater its immediacy. A tampered product that endangers customers' lives has greater immediacy than the initial complaint about moral violations by an activist group. A tampered product places people in immediate danger, whereas moral violations tend to be philosophical debates. Comparing two cases will clarify the idea of immediacy. In September 1990, Dayton Hudson Corporation withdrew its funding from Planned Parenthood. Women's groups were angered by the decision. Dayton had wanted to avoid being drawn into the abortion debate. Management felt that Planned Parenthood funding could tie them to abortion. Earlier in 1990, an anti-abortion group had urged Dayton to end its grant to Planned Parenthood (Kelly, 1990). Dayton officials had time to consider their options and study consumer attitudes. The grant was eventually restored. The moral debate did not require immediate action. In contrast, Burroughs Wellcome Company experienced extreme immediacy when two people in Washington state died from taking cyanide-laced Sudafed 12-hour capsules in March 1991. Burroughs had to get the product off the shelves and warn customers fast (Dagnoli & Colford, 1991; Kiley, 1991). The product safety concern did require immediate action.

Intense pressure from key stakeholders is another form of time pressure. When primary stakeholders (e.g., employees, customers, etc.) want action now, the crisis has immediacy. For example, the 1997 UPS drivers strike gave the crisis immediacy. UPS was delivering only 10% of its packages and losing millions of dollars (Sewell, 1997). A company cannot survive under such conditions. Pressure from employees gave the UPS crisis immediacy.

Uncertainty is the amount of ambiguity associated with a problem. The larger the amount of ambiguity surrounding a crisis, the greater its uncertainty. People are drawn to and have a need to reduce uncertainty. Organizations are no different (Dutton, 1986). Organizations need to know what is going on in their operations and why. How can a problem be corrected if it is not understood? Low uncertainty problems can be explained and corrected using common organizational rules and procedures. High uncertainty problems demand the type of extra attention crisis management can deliver. A comparison of similar crises with varying degrees of ambiguity helps to illustrate the power of ambiguity.

On December 10, 1995, American Airlines Flight 965 from Miami to Cali, Columbia, crashed into a mountain, killing 160 of the 164 people on board. On July 17, 1996, TWA Flight 800 from New York to Paris exploded 12 miles off the coast of Long Island, killing all 230 people on board. The Searchbank database listed five articles dedicated to Flight 965 and 141 for Flight 800. One reason for the different levels of media interest was ambiguity. For Flight 965, investigators quickly identified the automated guidance system as the cause of the crash. The final report, released 7 months later, confirmed the plane was following the wrong directional beacon, causing the automated guidance system to fly the plane into the side of a mountain (Dornheim, 1996; McGraw, 1996).

The cause of Flight 800's explosion was investigated and debated for more than 17 months. Missiles, terrorist bombs, lightening strikes, meteorites, and mechanical failures all surfaced as possible causes (Duffy & Beddingfield, 1996; Gray, 1996). The National Transportation Safety Board's final report ruled out all but mechanical failure. The evidence suggested that a small electrical charge ignited the fumes in an empty fuel tank that exploded and destroyed the plane. Flight 800 was a mystery because of the ambiguity surrounding the explosion. The mystery helped to hold media and public attention for more than a year. Furthermore, a Herculean effort went into discovering the mysterious cause of the explosion—reducing the ambiguity. Ambiguity demands to be resolved. Organizations must expend extra effort and resources when crisis ambiguity increases. The CMP delivers the attention required by an ambiguous crisis. The easiest crisis to sell is one that is perceived as very important, is very immediate, and has high uncertainty. Crisis managers must maximize as many of the crisis dimensions as possible when they frame the crisis for the dominant coalition.

Expertise of the Dominant Coalition

Organizational politics does creep into crisis management. Part of successful politicking is knowing the people with whom you are dealing. The management personnel who comprise the dominant coalition will possess varying types of expertise. Their expertise affects their comfort zone for dealing with problems. Managers like to successfully solve problems. Not surprisingly, they are more likely to be successful when dealing with problems within their expertise—their comfort zone. Comfort increases because they can identify more easily with the problem. Crisis managers must be sensitive to the expertise of the dominant coalition when framing a crisis.

The crisis frame should be adapted to the coalition by reflecting some aspect of their expertise (Dutton & Ashford, 1993). If the dominant coalition has financial expertise, the CMT should make sure the crisis frame includes a financial component. One way to tap expertise is to use jargon, the language of a profession. A message using jargon from the dominant coalition's area of expertise cultivates a sense of familiarity with the situation (Fairhurst & Sarr, 1996). Although not completely rational, the dominant coalition will want to manage crises they feel they can resolve successfully. A crisis leads stakeholders to question the dominant coalition's competence. Successful crisis management restores the perception of the dominant coalition's competence, whereas failure further erodes it (Dutton, 1986; Pearson & Clair, 1998). Hence, top management prefers crises they can feel comfortable with. The same holds true for prodromes. Any Dilbert cartoon will remind us that the organizational world does not run on pure logic.

Persuasiveness of the Presentation

Crisis managers will have an opportunity to convince the dominant coalition that a problem is a crisis. The crisis managers must use their persuasive skills when given the opportunity to argue for a crisis. People are persuaded by three basic factors: credibility, emotion, and reason (Larson 1989; Tan, 1985). Because the concept of credibility has already been described in detail, this section will apply the discussion to the challenge of selling crises to the dominant coalition. To be credible, the crisis managers need to have a record of successful task completion. Successful task completion demonstrates their expertise. Having a reputation as being honest works to enhance their trustworthiness (McCroskey, 1997).

Emotion centers on how the message is presented (McCroskey, 1997). To enhance the emotionality, a crisis should be presented in a dramatic fashion. A crisis is dramatic when it is novel. Vivid examples and stories help to create a dramatic presentation. The drama or emotion makes the message more interesting, easier to understand, and catches the attention of management (Dutton & Ashford, 1993; Larson, 1989). Management and other persuasive targets do not evaluate information on the basis of emotion alone; they also rely on logic.

Rational appeals stir our intellect (Larson, 1989). The use of facts (verifiable information) and logical evidence does act to persuade people. However, facts do not speak for themselves. Crisis managers can "spin" the facts by emphasizing the dangers of a situation. Lotteries sell tickets by telling people they cannot win if they do not play, not by reporting the odds against winning. Crisis managers would feature information that supports the strong likelihood and impact of a crisis while downplaying information that erodes either. Both sides of the issue must be presented because one-sided arguments are ineffective with educated audiences (Tan, 1985). Crisis managers who use emotions to capture the dominant coalition's attention must then use compelling rational evidence (i.e., statistics) to support the acceptance of the crisis (Dutton & Ashford, 1993). The message used to sell the crisis or prodrome should begin dramatically with vivid stories and examples and then move to reasoned arguments to reinforce its acceptance.

A hypothetical example demonstrates the use of emotion and reason. Imagine you work for Juice-Is-Us, a fresh vegetable juice maker. Evidence suggests that a recent shipment of tomato juice could be tainted with *E. coli*. You want to have the situation treated as a crisis. One option is to state the statistical probability of *E. coli* contamination and to note that the effects would be bad for the company. Another option is to describe in detail the effects of *E. coli* on the human body. Retell an actual case of a person who suffered from *E. coli*. Vivid examples and a story reinforce the dangers by bringing them to life. Next, note the possibility of people contracting the disease, not the probability they will not—spin the information. Add the possibility that regulatory agencies and law enforcement officials such as the FBI could investigate the situation. Finally, reinforce your case with statistics about the likelihood of contamination, the potential number of consumers affected, and the potential financial and reputational impact of any *E. coli* poisonings or deaths. The second option provides a much more persuasive argument for enacting the CMP.

Resistance to Crises

Not all problems can rise to the level of crisis in an organization. As stated in the opening of the chapter, crises can be contested, symbolic issues. Natural disasters, malevolence, technical and human breakdowns, megadamage, and workplace violence tend to be obvious crises in which most stakeholders would agree on the interpretation. Challenges and rumors are two crisis types in which contrasting interpretations abound. At least one stakeholder group will see a crisis, but the organization does not. The different interpretations can cause an organization to miss a crisis. It is foolish arrogance to believe that only the organization can place the crisis label to a situation. Crisis interpretations are socially created by primary stakeholders, secondary stakeholders (especially the news media), and the organization. If primary stakeholders believe a crisis exists, it does. Remember the Audi 5000 case from Chapter 4? Audi never did agree with the customers over the sudden acceleration problems with the 5000. The "crisis" generated years of bad press and consumer ill will before Audi recalled the 5000 (Sullivan, 1990; Versical, 1987).

Crisis managers should evaluate all stakeholder claims that a crisis exists. First, determine if the facts are correct—the claims are accurate. Inaccurate claims should be corrected, thereby diffusing the crisis. Second, if true, determine if other stakeholders will accept the interpretation of the situation as a crisis. Will more stakeholders in that group or other stakeholder groups support the crisis interpretation? In Audi's case, would more customers or government regulators see the sudden acceleration as a crisis? A crisis interpretation gains power and salience when it spreads among stakeholders. A crisis manager must decide if the values and interests embodied in the crisis interpretation will appeal to other stakeholders. Such decisions require a clear understanding of one's stakeholders.

Philip Morris ended a billboard advertising campaign due to fear of a spreading crisis interpretation. In 1990, Philip Morris was challenged for having a high number of billboards selling cigarettes in inner-city areas. The crisis interpretation painted Philip Morris as a racist organization that exploited minorities in the inner city. About 40 different demonstrations were launched against Philip Morris by Rev. Calvin Butts, an inner-city antitobacco advocate. Philip Morris was worried about being labeled a racist organization that exploits minorities. Philip Morris agreed to reduce the number of cigarette billboards in inner-city areas and to join a council that would examine outdoor advertising practices in inner-city areas (Fahey & Dagnoli, 1990). If crisis managers believe a crisis interpretation will resonate with other stakeholders, they must work to convince the dominant coalition to accept it as a crisis.

Another time a crisis is missed is when the dominant coalition purposefully refuses to see a crisis. Embezzlement is a common crisis that is purposefully not seen. Even when internal or external audits discover embezzlement, most organizations hide it. The FBI believes that only 10% of all embezzlements are reported. Embezzlement is embarrassing, and many organizations fear that reporting it will encourage more theft or anger shareholders, clients, or customers (Strauss, 1998). Each organization and industry has its own type of crises that are purposefully ignored. The organization may take actions to address the problem but chooses to keep the situation quiet and avoid involving most stakeholders. The organization is engaging in a form of cover-up. Any type of cover-up is dangerous because it could be exposed later and trigger a different and more severe crisis (Barton, 1993).

Crisis managers can affect the acceptance or rejection of a crisis by how they frame it when they present it to the dominant coalition. Crisis managers must have information to support the frame and articulate it in a compelling fashion. Frame development begins with information. Crisis managers need information that indicates a crisis is (a) important—the damage will occur or become more severe by spreading; (b) immediate—there are pressures to act now; or (c) uncertain—there is ambiguity surrounding the situation. Crisis managers should consider the dominant coalition's expertise and basic elements of persuasion when selling the frame. The dominant coalition must be familiar and comfortable with the crisis—see it as within their realm of expertise. Jargon is one way to link a crisis to the dominant coalition's expertise. Vivid stories and examples serve to capture the dominant coalition's attention. The facts about the importance, immediacy, and uncertainty of the crisis are then offered to support the acceptance of the crisis label.

Organizations can be blind to crises. It falls to the crisis manager to "cure the blindness" by convincing management to openly acknowledge a situation as a crisis. Crisis managers should sell a crisis because they believe enacting the CMP will improve the situation and benefit the organization and its stakeholders. Selling crises is even more difficult when the dominant coalition is purposefully ignoring the crisis. This section offers resources and techniques crisis managers can use to sell crises. The probability of successfully selling the crisis is enhanced when crisis managers take the time to build and present compelling crisis frames. Organizations can be blind to prodromes as well. For instance, a semiconductor manufacturer ignored for 8 years evidence that its lax operating procedures were poisoning workers. Finally, a lawsuit by 30 workers alleging widespread ills and workplace abuses brought the problem to light. The case was settled out of court (Smith, 1998). The recommendations for selling crises can also be applied to selling prodromes.

APPLICATION POINT

This section provides guidelines for helping crisis managers to sell crises and prodromes to the dominant coalition. Now is your

chance to apply those guidelines. Two different cases are provided
for you to practice framing crises or prodromes.

Case 1: Selling a Crisis

*You are on the CMT for the U.S. division of a large multinational
corporation. Among the products made by your division is a disposable
butane lighter. Your lighters have always conformed to accepted safety
standards. However, from 1994 to 1996, there were reports of your
lighter exploding. Your competitors experienced similar complaints. The
lighter was redesigned for 1997. The old lighter could fail to extinguish
completely after use, then explode moments later. People can and were
badly burned from lighters exploding in their pockets. A total of 147
exploding-lighter lawsuits have been filed against your company; one
involved a death. You have learned that the New York Times and a major
network news show are collecting information about the exploding
lighters. Over the past 3 years, the dominant coalition has shown no
interest in the problem. Outline how you would frame this crisis for the
dominant coalition. The dominant coalition's backgrounds are in engineering and finance. Identify your key selling points and explain why
each is important to selling the crisis.*

Case 2: Selling a Prodrome

*You are on the CMT of a large U.S. corporation. One of its holdings is
a tobacco company that makes and markets cigarettes. Your company
has plans to launch a new cigarette next month, the Montana. The target
market are women, 18 to 20 years old, no education beyond high school,
and who are unemployed or part-time workers. You see the Montana as
a prodrome. Public opinion, including that of your stockholders, is
against targeting a young, unsophisticated audience. The government
and antitobacco groups are waiting for any little mistake to attack the
tobacco industry. You believe the Montana will bring condemnations
from antismoking groups and government officials. Lesser actions by
other tobacco companies have triggered just such hostile reactions. The
negative publicity could hurt your stock prices and bring closer government scrutiny of your tobacco company. Outline how you would frame
this prodrome for the dominant coalition. The dominant coalition's*

*background is in food manufacturing. Identify your key selling points
and explain why each is important to selling the prodrome.*

Crises and Information Needs

Crises can be regarded as "information-poor" situations. A typical crisis
situation requires large amounts of information because initially little is
known; it is a rapidly changing situation, or the changes in the crisis situation
are more random than predictable. Any or all of these factors indicate that
the information demands of a crisis are complex (Barge, 1994). In turn, there
is pressure on a crisis team to acquire and process information quickly and
accurately if it is to operate effectively in a crisis. Understanding and coping
with the information demands of a crisis is part of crisis management.

Crises as Information Processing

Earlier, the work of Egelhoff and Sen (1992) was noted for its concern
about information processing. They identified information processing as a
major task during crisis management. Crisis managers begin with the unknown—the crisis. To make a crisis known, crisis managers must collect
crisis-relevant information. Crisis-related information is raw data about the
crisis. Before this information is useful, it must be processed. Crisis managers
must examine and interpret the raw data. The processed information allows
the crisis managers to make sense of the crisis—the crisis becomes known.
From the processed information, crisis managers make decisions about what
actions to take and what messages to communicate to stakeholders (Barge,
1994; Clampitt, 1991). Crisis management is a process of moving from the
unknown to the known through information gathering and processing.

A sample crisis illustrates the process of moving from the unknown to the
known. There is an explosion in an aerosol can facility. Among what the crisis
team knows includes the following: the location of the explosion, the employees working in the area at the time, the chemicals involved in the process,
and the exact tasks performed in the area of the explosion. What the crisis
team does not know but needs to know includes who was injured, the nature
and severity of the injuries, emergency actions taken after the explosion,
amount of damage to the facility, the need to suspend operations, and
possible causes of the explosion. The crisis team collects information until
it has the requisite information about the crisis.

The Unknown

The crisis begins with a trigger event or someone convincing management that a crisis exists. Either way, the organization is faced with a problem that now commands the crisis team's attention and demands some resolution. The first task of the CMT is to determine what it needs to know about the crisis, what it already knows, and what it does not know. What it needs to know is the information the crisis team requires to enact the CMP and make decisions. What is already known would be the pregathered crisis information or the crisis data bank. What the team does not know is the difference between what is needed and what exists in the crisis data bank. Understanding the three informational concerns allows the crisis team to determine what information is needed to cope with the crisis. The team then must try to reduce what it does not know by collecting crisis-relevant information.

Information Gathering

Information gathering should be an organized search, not a wild scavenger hunt. The crisis team must prioritize the information needs, know where to go, and know who to ask to collect the information (Clampitt, 1991). Information needs are not equal. The crisis team must prioritize the information it needs. High-priority information needs should receive immediate attention and greater effort. For example, during an industrial accident that vents dangerous gas, the crisis team must know the direction and intensity of the gas cloud before it worries about the cause of the gas venting. Each crisis will determine its own information priorities.

Knowing you need certain information is pointless if the team does not know where to get it. Links to organizational members and external stakeholders become valuable when a crisis team requires information because the links are the sources for the requisite information (Pearson & Clair, 1998). It behooves a crisis team to know the sources of potential crisis-relevant information before a crisis hits. The idea of developing crisis information networks will be discussed shortly.

Information Processing: The Known

"Raw" information is a starting point, not an end point, when trying to understand a crisis. The crisis team must take the information it has gathered and process it. Information processing involves attending to and interpreting the information (Clampitt, 1991; Weick, 1979). The crisis team must determine what these pieces of information mean. What we typically call making sense out of information is information processing. By processing the information, the team determines if it actually has assembled the information it needed. Only by analyzing information can a team determine if enough information of the requisite kind has been collected to convert the unknown into the known. The crisis managers must determine if they have enough information to make effective decisions. If information is lacking, information gathering continues. If there is enough information, decisions are made about what the organization will do and what it will say about the crisis, the domain of Chapter 7.

Information-Processing Problems

The crisis management writings treat information processing as a rather simple task. Crisis managers are told to mobilize their resources and gather all possible information (Mitchell, 1986). We are led to believe that information is easy to collect and analyze. However, this is not the case. Research in organizational and small group communication has found consistent flaws that plague information collecting and processing (Pace & Boren, 1973; Stohl & Redding, 1987). By understanding these flaws, we can construct better mechanisms for crisis team information collecting and processing. Crisis managers should be aware of five flaws: serial reproduction errors, MUM effect, message overload, information acquisition biases, and group decision-making errors.

Serial Reproduction Errors

Have you ever received a message that has traveled through three or four different people before reaching you? The odds are that the message made little sense or was far from accurate. This distortion is known as the serial reproduction problem or serial transmission effect. The more people a messages passes through before reaching its final destination, the greater the likelihood of the message being distorted (Daniels et al., 1997). Obviously, inaccurate information is problematic during a crisis. It leads to public embarrassment through misstatements to the media and dangerous miscues by a crisis team that has based its decisions on inaccurate information. Crisis teams must collect and store accurate information about the progression of events in a crisis because such documentation is central to postcrisis evaluation, crisis-related lawsuits, and governmental investigations triggered by the crisis.

MUM Effect

One critical source of crisis-related information would be members of the organization. The MUM effect acts to block the flow of negative or unpleasant information in an organization (Tesser & Rosen, 1975). Not surprisingly, people in organizations have a tendency to withhold negative information completely (e.g., information that makes them look bad) or alter the information to make it less damaging (Stohl & Redding, 1987). Crises involve negative situations. Things have gone wrong and threaten the organization in some way (Barton, 1993). Organizational members may be reluctant to provide negative information, especially if it could make them or their organizational unit look bad. Some attribute the explosion of the space shuttle *Challenger* to the MUM effect (Goldhaber, 1990).

The night before the *Challenger* launch, 15 engineers at Morton Thiokol argued against the launch. Morton Thiokol makes the solid rocket boosters (SRBs) that help to lift the space shuttle into orbit. The SRBs have O-rings, rubber circles that seal gaps and prevent improper ignition of the solid fuels. The O-rings have no backup. If an O-ring fails, the solid rocket fuel can ignite improperly, explode, and destroy the vehicle. Everyone at NASA was aware of what would happen if an O-ring failed. The engineers felt that the weather was too cold and would prevent the O-rings from functioning properly. (O-ring failure was determined to be the cause of the explosion.) Morton Thiokol originally refused to okay the launch. After another meeting, the decision was reversed, and Morton Thiokol approved the launch. Middle managers at NASA never told either Arnold Aldrich, the manager of the entire space shuttle program, or Jesse Moore, NASA's associate administrator responsible for the final launch decision, about Morton Thiokol's launch concerns (Boffey, 1986; Mecham, 1986; Sanger, 1986). It is all speculation if either of these two men would have stopped the launch had they known about Morton Thiokol's concerns. However, NASA managers illustrated the MUM effect by not relaying negative information to their superiors. No crisis teams can afford to have negative information withheld or modified just to make it more pleasant or to protect team members.

Message Overload

A common problem experienced by people in organizations is message overload—people receiving too much information too quickly (Stohl & Redding, 1987). The risk of information overload is great during a crisis.

As noted earlier, crises are information poor—an information vacuum—that demands the collecting and processing of large amounts of information to compensate for this information void. The demand for information should produce a vast flow of data going into the crisis team. However, the danger is that the information flow becomes problematic due to overload instead of helping to close the gap between the unknown and the known in the crisis.

Information Acquisition Bias

Because available information exceeds the human ability to "make sense" of it, people naturally have selective perceptions. Selective perception means that we each focus on certain aspects of the information we encounter and disregard the rest (Barge, 1994). The risk in crisis management is as follows. Early on in the crisis, crisis team members form impressions about the nature of the crisis. All subsequent information is tested against this initial perception. The crisis team will seek information that confirms the initial impression while discounting information that contradicts this impression. Unfortunately, the initial perception may blind the crisis team to critical crisis-related information needed for its decision-making efforts. Another risk arises when members define any new crisis in terms of past crises (Barge, 1994). Rather than treating a new crisis as a novel event, it is simply viewed as a version of some previous crisis. If the past crisis is a poor match to the current crisis, the crisis team applies the wrong template when it addresses the new crisis. The crisis team manages the wrong crisis because it mistakenly manages the old crisis and not the current one. In either instance, important nuances about the current crisis are lost. The crisis team discounts potentially important information because of the blinders from initial impressions or baggage from past crises.

The two information acquisition biases can be demonstrated by returning to the case of TWA Flight 800 discussed earlier. Initial reports indicated that a terrorist bomb was responsible for the incident. The pattern of the blast and discovery of microscopic PETN, a plastic explosive, traces on salvaged pieces of the plane were the best evidence. Investigators could have examined only the circumstantial evidence suggesting a bomb—the initial perceptions. The remainder of the investigation could have ignored all other possible causes. Another reason to suspect terrorism was the similarity to the Pan Am Flight 103 bombing over Lockerbie, Scotland, in 1988. The radar tapes and the voice and flight data recordings of Flight 800 were very similar to Flight 103's. Investigators could have examined all the remaining evidence through the previous crisis. As it turns out, Pan Am Flight 103 was the wrong template for TWA Flight 800 (Gray, 1996; Watson, 1996). Had either of these information acquisition biases been used, the investigators would have ignored the clues to the real cause of the explosion, mechanical failure.

Group Decision-Making Errors

Groups are prone to decision-making errors when they fail to use critical thinking skills. Critical thinking is a process of carefully evaluating information (Williams & Olaniran, 1994). Two tendencies contribute to poor group decision making. First, the group fails to see a problem or identify the correct cause of the problem. The group is led to ignore problems or solve the wrong problems. Second, the group improperly evaluates its alternatives for solving a problem (Hirokawa & Rost, 1992). Improper evaluation can lead the group to select an ineffective alternative for solving the problem. Both types of errors result in poor decision making by a group. In each instance, the root cause of the error can be traced to the careless handling of information.

Summary

The purpose for reviewing information-gathering and processing errors was twofold. First, the errors highlight how difficult information gathering and processing can be. Crisis team members should not underestimate these problems. Second, realization of the problems can help to develop more effective information-gathering and processing mechanisms for crisis teams. Information gathering and processing should become more effective when the crisis team is trying to counter the information-gathering and processing errors.

APPLICATION POINT

Information processing demands that a crisis manager be able to assess the information demands of a situation. Two cases are offered for practicing your information-processing skills.

▓ Case 1: The Explosion

You are on the CMT of a moderate-sized U.S. chemical manufacturing company. During the night shift, an explosion shook your fertilizer manufacturing facility near Wooster, Ohio. You learn the following when you arrive on the scene: One person is confirmed dead, six people are confirmed injured, and around five people are missing. Firefighters are on the scene, along with your hazardous materials team. What else does the CMT need to know to manage the explosion crisis? What sources are likely to have the needed information? On a sheet of paper, list all the important facts you need on the left side and the possible sources for the information on the right side. Briefly explain why each fact is on your list.

▓ Case 2: The EPA Lawsuit

You are on the CMT of a large timber and paper company based in the United States. The Environmental Protection Agency (EPA) files a $40 million lawsuit, alleging that 11 of your company's wood-processing plants in the South are illegally polluting the air with ozone. The EPA claims that your company violated the 1990 Clean Air Act by failing to provide accurate reports of its airborne emissions of ozone-forming compounds. A quick review of your own clean-air audits suggests that there may be some truth to the charges. What else does the CMT need to know to manage the lawsuit crisis? What sources are likely to have the needed information? On a sheet of paper, list all the important facts you need on the left side and the possible sources for the information on the right side. Briefly explain why each fact is on your list.

Information-Processing Mechanisms

Information-processing mechanisms are designed to aid crisis teams in both collecting and processing crisis-relevant information. The information-processing mechanisms involve both structural and procedural elements. The structural elements focus on how to collect information. The procedural elements center on how to prevent or reduce processing errors.

Structural Elements

Crisis managers need to access sources that have information they might need during a crisis. Crisis managers will seek out the needed information that is not a part of their crisis database—the pregathered information collected for crisis management purposes (Fearn-Banks, 1996). Communication consultants recognize the value of networks when collecting information. Networks are your relationships with other people. Stronger networks lead to better information gathering and more accurate understanding of problems (Barge, 1994; Clampitt, 1991). CMTs must develop connections they can use to collect crisis-related information. I will call the system the *crisis information network*. The crisis information network is composed of external and internal stakeholder networks. In addition to soliciting information, the crisis team must evaluate the information it receives. Both the development of networks and procedures for evaluating information are valuable aids to information gathering. No crisis team can be effective without sufficient information for decision making (Hirokawa & Keyton, 1995).

Internal Stakeholder Network. The internal stakeholder network is composed of the people within the crisis team's organization. The foundation of the internal stakeholder network stems from the networks of the individual team members. Their contacts and information sources become the team's sources. The crisis team then looks to expand the list. The expansion can be accomplished by asking each contact for others who may know about the subject (Barge, 1994). The crisis team should formalize the information by developing a list of contacts for various types of information that might be needed during a crisis. The crisis team develops an internal stakeholder section for the crisis information network directory. The crisis information network directory lists multiple contacts for various types of information the team may need and can be an appendix to the CMP or a separate document from the CMP. The crisis information network directory sheet starts with a listing of the expertise required. The expertise required is a way of categorizing people by the type of information they possess. The expertise designation is followed by basic contact information: name, organization and title, phone number, pager number, fax number, and e-mail. Multiple contact points are important because if one fails, another can be tried until the person is contacted.

External Stakeholder Network. The external stakeholder network is composed of all nonemployees of the crisis team's organization. Common members would include customers, government officials, suppliers, distributors, community members, competitors, and investors (Pearson & Mitroff, 1993).

Any external stakeholder could be a part of this network. The secondary contact sheet from the CMP is an essential resource. The secondary contact sheet provides contact people for all stakeholders—it indicates who in the organization handles each particular stakeholder. The crisis team converts the information from the secondary contact sheet into an external stakeholder section for the crisis information network directory. The structure of the external section parallels the internal section. The difference is that the external section would include the contact person(s) for the various stakeholders. The crisis team would have the option of direct contact with the external stakeholder or the use of the organization's contact person(s). A contact person is helpful when a positive relationship has been established. The stakeholder should be more open with the contact person given the history of having a positive relationship with that person versus the potential of having no relational history with a member of the crisis team. The open relationship should make it easier for the contact person to solicit higher-quality information from the external stakeholder.

Crisis Information Logs. During a crisis, it is critical to track the amount and movement of crisis-related information within the organization. Crisis information logs are a useful tool for monitoring crisis information flow. Logs record when a crisis team member makes an information request and the result of that request. By logging its information requests and receipt, the crisis team knows what information it has and what information it still needs. The log starts with the standard concerns: the time and date of the request, requested from whom, the channel used to make the request, and requested by whom. Once the information is received, the time, date, channel used to deliver the information, and source are recorded along with the name of the person who received the information.

The next step is to evaluate and process the information. Team members must decide if any follow-up information is needed or if the received information is sufficient. The log notes when the information was processed and by whom. Accepted criteria for evaluating information are clarity, timeliness, and depth. Clarity means that the information has one interpretation, not multiple interpretations, and that people can easily understand what the message means. Timeliness means that the information is current and received when needed. Depth means that the information seems complete—it answers the questions asked (Barge, 1994). A hypothetical example will demonstrate clarity, timeliness, and depth. Imagine a hurricane hits the central manufacturing facility of your power tool manufacturing company.

The CMT wants to know when operations will resume. Does your CMT want to hear "in a reasonable amount of time" (lack of clarity) or "in 5 to 6 days" (clarity)? The CMT needs to know what alternatives are available for maintaining production. Does your CMT want a business resumption plan that has not been revised in 3 years (not timely) or a current business resumption plan (timely)? Finally, the CMT needs to know about injured workers who were on duty when the hurricane struck. Does your CMT want to learn there were 10 injuries (lack of depth) or the exact names of those injured and the extent of their injuries (depth)? The CMT works best when it receives quality information.

Precision should be stressed in the logs. The information is to be recorded as it is received and not summarized or modified. Precise written records help to eliminate some of the factors that promote serial reproduction errors. Also, having a written record reduces the number of sources used to transmit a message, which again serves to reduce the likelihood of serial reproduction errors.

The crisis information log records when information is requested, when it is received, and if it has been processed. Time and date help to assess the timeliness of information. Channels are useful in evaluation. It can help to determine the extent to which specific channels were effective in requesting and sending information. Noting who the information was requested from will help to determine if better sources could be used in the future. The source of the information indicates the believability of the information due in part to the credibility of the source. The log also tracks if, when, and by whom the information was processed. Overall, the log helps the crisis team to monitor its information collection and processing efforts.

Procedural Efforts

The procedural efforts are all actions that can be taken to combat various information-processing problems. A priority system is one way to combat information overload. A priority system uses selective criteria to establish the perceived importance of information (Stohl & Redding, 1987). Prioritization is a multistepped process involving evaluation, storage, and retrieval. When incoming information is logged, it is also evaluated. A simple priority system might use three categories: immediate, routine, and miscellaneous. Immediate is information the crisis team requires for pressing decisions or actions. Routine is the basic information a crisis team typically needs during the course of a crisis management effort. Miscellaneous is information that is received, has no apparent value, but does have some relationship to the crisis.

Routine and miscellaneous information is stored until the crisis has time for or need of it. Information might be stored on paper and/or in computer files. Retrieval involves extracting the desired information from the information queue. Storage and retrieval require categorizing the information by topic. The information is assigned a general topic area and a list of key subjects it covers. The process is similar to cataloging books in a library. Chapter 8 provides additional information on storage and retrieval.

Allowing the crisis team to focus on the high-priority information reduces the message load, thereby decreasing information overload. The message priority system should reflect the crisis team's information needs. A contaminated food recall crisis will illustrate and clarify the priority process. Top priorities at the start of a food recall include (a) identifying affected consumers, (b) locating the source of the contamination, and (c) informing consumers about the recall. Information related to any of these three topics would be categories as immediate during the initial phase of the crisis. Suppose the crisis team received the following information:

1. results of production facility inspections,
2. newspaper stories about the company's crisis management efforts,
3. projected costs of the recall,
4. confirmation that the recall information is being reported in the news media,
5. projections on lost market share,
6. estimated recovery time,
7. confirmed cases of consumer illnesses,
8. consumer reactions to the recall, and
9. Internet newsgroup discussion linking the recall to a government conspiracy.

Information chunks 1 (inspection results), 4 (confirmation of recall in the news media), and 7 (cases of illness) would be immediate priority. In each case, the information relates directly to the initial priorities of the crisis team. Information chunks 2, 3, 5, 6, and 8 would be routine priority. Eventually the crisis team will need to assess the financial damage (2 and 5), project recovery time (6), and evaluate its crisis management performance (2 and 8). Information chunk 9 is miscellaneous because there probably is no government conspiracy here, but the information does pertain to the crisis. When incoming information is heavy and the risk of information overload is high, crisis teams would benefit from an information priority system.

APPLICATION POINT

Now it is your turn to develop a priority system. Select two crisis types from Chapter 5. For each crisis, create an information priority system to be used during the initial phase of the crisis. Think about what information is critical at the start of each crisis. Be sure to carefully define each of the categories in your priority system. Next, compare the priority systems—how are they alike and different? What accounts for the similarities and differences?

Data splitting is a technique used to combat information acquisition bias. Data splitting divides information into smaller units for more effective analysis. Instead of one big block of information, there are smaller units of information. The crisis team can examine smaller units of information more carefully because the smaller units are easier to examine in detail. In addition, smaller units act to break patterns that could feed into preexisting information-processing biases (Barge, 1994). Let us return to the TWA Flight 800 case. Data splitting would include considering the flight data and radar records separately before placing each into the larger picture of the investigation.

Unfortunately, there is no simple technique for handling the MUM effect. The only proven means is an open communication system. In an open communication system, people engage in the candid disclosure and receipt of facts, even if it is bad news (Redding, 1972). Openness is developed through trust and past interactions with one another (Barge, 1994). The crisis team members must work to earn the trust of organizational members and demonstrate there will not be negative sanctions for passing along information that indicates member mistakes or errors. Furthermore, positive relationships with external stakeholders facilitate the flow of accurate information from outside sources. A positive relationship is built on openness (Grunig, 1992).

Group decision-making errors can be combated through vigilance and the devil's advocate technique. The discussion of crisis team selection touched on vigilance, a form of critical thinking. The primary elements of vigilance are (a) problem analysis, (b) standards for evaluating alternative choices, (c) understanding the important positive aspects of an alternative choice, and (d) understanding the important negative aspects of an alternative choice. The four elements serve to counter the two group decision-making errors. Problem analysis counters the failure of the group to identify the correct cause of the problem, whereas standards for evaluating alternative choices, understanding the important positive aspects of alternative choice, and understanding the important negative aspects of an alternative choice all serve to compensate for the group improperly evaluating alternatives for solving the problem (Hirokawa & Rost, 1992). The devil's advocate technique makes sure that some group member always voices opposition to a group's plan. The opposition is supposed to lead the group to reevaluate its decisions and reminds the group to examine weaknesses it may have glossed over originally (Barge, 1994).

Conclusion

A crisis cannot be managed effectively if the organization is blind to its details. At times, crisis team members will have to sell a crisis to the dominant coalition before action can be taken to resolve the crisis. This chapter began by offering suggestions for crisis selling. Once its existence is recognized, information collection and processing are vital to the successful management of a crisis. Crisis teams need accurate and timely information if they are to make effective decisions quickly. Although it sounds easy, numerous problems can hinder information gathering and processing. The chapter ended by reviewing the main problems that can affect information gathering and processing. Moreover, suggestions have been made for procedures and techniques CMTs can adopt to improve their information-gathering and processing capabilities. Taken together, the information in this chapter prepares the crisis team for identifying the crisis and processing the information needed to resolve the crisis. Chapter 7 will begin to develop how the information collected by the crisis team is translated into organizational action.

7

Crisis Containment
and Recovery

Once a crisis hits, the crisis team must work (a) to prevent it from spreading to unaffected areas of the organization or the environment and (b) to limit its duration (Mitroff, 1994). Communication presents unique challenges during the containment and recovery phases. Stakeholders must be informed about the crisis. Actions must be taken to address the crisis. The organization's progress toward recovery must be reported. This chapter is concerned with how communication is used to achieve crisis containment and recovery. Key elements of any containment and recovery are perceptions of control and compassion. The crisis team must prove to stakeholders that it is in control of the crisis, and the team must remember to show concern for victims (Frank, 1994; Mitchell, 1986). The control and compassion factors place particular demands on crisis communication.

Four distinct topics must be addressed in containment and recovery: initial response, reputational management concerns, enactment of the contingency and business resumption plan, and follow-up communication. Crisis communication to stakeholders begins with the initial response to the crisis. The initial response is important because it sets the tone for the rest of the crisis. Reputational damage is always a concern with a crisis. Crisis communication can be used to limit or even lessen the reputational threat of a crisis (Coombs & Holladay, 1996). Stakeholders must know when the organization will resume normal operations and what contingencies are in place until the return to normal operations has been announced (Barton, 1995). Stakehold-ers need to know if a facility is closed, when and if it will reopen, and where to go if an alternative site is being used. Such information directly affects employees, suppliers, and clients (Myers, 1993). Finally, the crisis team must engage in follow-up communication with stakeholders. Stakeholders must be updated about crisis developments, and the crisis team must answer new inquiries as well. Communication is essential to the execution of all four elements of containment and recovery.

Initial Crisis Response

The initial response is mentioned more frequently in the crisis management writings than any other topic. The initial response represents the first public statements the spokesperson makes about the crisis. The initial statement typically is delivered through the mass media, hence the concern in crisis management with media relations (e.g., Barton, 1993; Fearn-Banks, 1996; Lerbinger, 1997; Seitel, 1983). The focus on initial response stems from the fact that first impressions form quickly and color the remainder of the crisis communication efforts with stakeholders (Sen & Egelhoff, 1991). Crisis managers are encouraged to be quick, consistent, open, sympathetic, and informative. The quick, consistent, and open recommendations involve form—how a crisis response should be presented. Informative and sympa-thetic impressions represent content—the actual messages contained in the crisis response.

Respond Quickly

The terms *quick* and *quickly* are synonymous with initial response. The need for speed in crisis communication continues to escalate as technology accelerates the spread of information, thereby actually reducing the amount of time a crisis team has for responding (Barton, 1993). The media report about a crisis very quickly. In some cases, the crisis spokesperson learns about the crisis from media reports before being officially notified, creating a bad situation for the organization. The quicker the stakeholders hear about a crisis, the quicker the crisis team must respond to the crisis. Obviously speed increases risks. The primary risk associated with speed would be the potential for inaccuracies (Smith & Hayne, 1997). Because the crisis team must act quickly, it can make mistakes. Johnson & Johnson committed a "quickness" mistake when handling the original Tylenol product tampering. In 1982, seven people in the Chicago area died from taking cyanide-laced Extra-Strength Tylenol capsules. A reporter asked if cyanide was used in the Tylenol manufacturing facility. The Johnson & Johnson spokesperson initially said there was no cyanide in the plant that produced Tylenol. The statement was in error. The testing laboratories at the production facility did use cyanide. At the time of the press conference, the spokesperson did not have all the relevant information. The error was corrected as soon as it was discovered (Berg & Robb, 1992; Leon, 1983; Snyder, 1983). However, speed does not have to mean mistakes, and the benefits of a quick initial response far outweigh the risks.

Throughout this book a crisis has been viewed as an event that triggers a need for information. Chapter 6 examined the crisis team's need for information. Simultaneous with crisis team information needs are stakeholder information needs. It is accurate to say that a crisis creates an information void. Nature abhors a vacuum. Any information void will be filled somehow and by someone. The media have deadlines, so they are driven to fill the information void quickly. The media demands trigger a chain reaction effect. The media are going to report on a crisis. Most stakeholders seeking to fill the information void will use the media as their primary or initial source of crisis-related information (Fearn-Banks, 1996). If the crisis team does not supply the initial crisis information to the media, some other group will. The other groups may be ill informed, misinformed, or out to get the organization. The information void can become filled with rumor and speculation, not facts (Caruba, 1994). Whatever the case, the initial crisis information will be incorrect and may intensify the damage created by the crisis. A quick response helps to ensure that stakeholders receive accurate crisis-related information.

Silence is a very passive response. The use of silence reflects uncertainty and passivity by the organization. Passiveness is the exact opposite perception an organization should be attempting to create. The silence response suggests that an organization is not in control and is not trying to take control of how it or the crisis is perceived by stakeholders (Hearit, 1994). Because silence allows others to take control of the situation (Brummett, 1980), other groups define the crisis for stakeholders. A quick response is necessary to get the organization's definition of the crisis—its side of the story—into the media and out to the stakeholders (Heath, 1994; Kempner, 1995). A quick response also helps to create the impression of control. When an organization responds quickly, the crisis team appears to be in control or gaining control of the situation (Kempner, 1995; Mitchell, 1986). A quick response demonstrates that the organization is taking action and is capable of responding to a crisis (Darling, 1994; Maynard, 1993). Conversely, a slow response makes an organization appear to be incompetent (Donath, 1984). Control is important to credibility; it is part of the organization's expertise. A crisis indicates a lack of control in and by the organization (Heath, 1994). A quick response is a first step in reasserting organizational control and reestablishing organizational credibility (Augustine, 1995).

There are limits to being able to respond quickly. In some crises, it takes time to collect and process the necessary information. Large-scale accidents produce great confusion. A January 1998 explosion at a Sierra Chemical dynamite manufacturing facility 10 miles east of Reno, Nevada, exemplifies the limits to quickness. Initial reports on January 7 listed eight injured, three known dead, and two missing. A report later that same day listed six injured, five missing, and no confirmed deaths. The next day, officials had the final count: six injured and four missing who were presumed to be dead. Apparently, one of the five people originally listed as missing had not reported to work on January 7 ("Five Missing," 1998; "Four Missing," 1998; "Nevada Explosion," 1998). It takes time to collect some types of information.

A crisis team might have to go before the media with an incomplete story. That is okay. There is no crisis management sin in telling the media that the team does not know something but will provide the information as soon as possible. Consider a variation to the Sierra Chemical case. The Sierra Chemical crisis team delays a press conference until it has all of the information about the explosion. In the meantime, the local news media are telling people about suspected causes. Perhaps a disgruntled former employee claims that the accident was due to mismanagement. Mismanagement is the explanatory theme reported as a likely cause of the blast because no other reasons are forthcoming. The initial news stories will have Sierra Chemical responsible for the workers' deaths and injuries. This theme frames the thinking of reporters and other stakeholders. Speculation and rumor inadvertently become crisis fact. Better to have the spokesperson saying that the cause is still under investigation than stakeholders being fed inaccurate causes.

Lack of information can begat two sins. The first sin is "no comment." For years, crisis spokespersons have been told not to say "no comment" (Mitchell, 1986; Kempner, 1995). The danger is that stakeholders hear "we're guilty" instead of "no comment." Better to say the information is not yet available but will be sent to the media when it is received. This brings up the second sin: not delivering on the information promised to the media (Birch, 1994; Gonzalez-Herrero & Pratt, 1995). A good organization-media relationship is built on trust. Trust requires an organization to deliver on its promises. Failure to provided promised information damages the organization-media relationship, thereby eroding the organization's credibility with the media.

Speak With One Voice: Consistency

The organization must deliver consistent messages to stakeholders. A unified response promotes consistency. Consistency does not mean having just one person who speaks for the organization every time there is a public statement, as some crisis experts recommend (Carney & Jorden, 1993). Rather, speaking with one voice means coordinating the efforts of the official spokespersons and discouraging other organizational members from becoming unofficial spokespersons (Seitel, 1983). Chapter 5 detailed this point in the spokesperson discussion. The crisis team must ensure that the team of spokespersons is well prepared because preparation promotes consistency in their responses. Spokespersons sharing the same information base will be more consistent than those who do not.

There is no way to ensure the consistency or accuracy of messages from unofficial spokespersons. The unofficial spokespersons can be any employee the media happen to persuade to answer questions. The crisis management plan (CMP) specifies the process for handling inquiries. The process should be reinforced to employees so that they fight the urge to speak for the company. It is hard for employees to resist the opportunity to be on the local news. A camera crew appears as an employee is leaving work. The employee has a chance to be on television. Why not comment on the crisis? Most employees are not aware of the perils of talking to reporters thirsty for a scoop. Again, speculation and rumor enter the media through comments made by unofficial spokespersons. The CMP and crisis training can help to alleviate this problem. Consistency is essential to building the credibility of the response. A consistent message is more believable than an inconsistent one (Clampitt, 1991; Garvin, 1996).

Openness

The openness of the organization is really a multifaceted concept. Openness means (a) availability to the media, (b) willingness to disclose information, and (c) honesty. Availability means that a spokesperson will answer inquiries in a timely fashion or immediately if the information is available. In a crisis, the focus is on the media, but other stakeholders may ask or demand that their questions be answered. Neighbors of a facility may want to know how a chemical leak might affect them, or stockholders might want to know the financial impact of the crisis. The foundation for availability should have been developed as part of relationship building (refer to Chapter 4 for detailed information on relationship building). The organization should have a history of being responsive to the needs of stakeholders. During a crisis, this responsiveness takes the form of spokespersons making every reasonable attempt to respond to questions promptly. *Reasonable* is an important qualifier. Sometimes the situation does not allow for an immediate response. When delays are necessary, tell stakeholders why the question cannot be answered and when they might be able to expect a response (Stewart & Cash, 1997). Never let a request go unacknowledged, or you risk damaging the stakeholder-organization relationship. Communication with stakeholders is a two-way process. You must honor their requests if you expect them to accept the organization's messages.

A typical struggle in crisis management is between the legal perspective for limited disclosure of crisis-related information and the public relations perspective for full disclosure of crisis-related information (Fitzpatrick & Rubin, 1995; Kaufmann, Kesner, & Hazen, 1994; Twardy, 1994; Tyler, 1997). The choice actually is on a continuum between saying as little as possible (limited disclosure) or revealing everything the organization knows about the crisis (full disclosure). Cautious full disclosure is preached heavily in crisis management circles (Kaufmann et al., 1994). However, full disclosure is rarely always possible or advisable. Some crisis-related information may be proprietary, covered by privacy laws, involve company policies, or be sensitive. This means some information cannot be disseminated publicly. At other times, full disclosure could exacerbate a crisis by escalating the direct and indirect costs of litigation. Direct costs involve the amount of money awarded to plaintiffs, and indirect costs represent trial costs, personnel matters, lost work time by executives, deaths, serious injuries, and possible regulatory changes (Kaufmann et al., 1994). Organizations do have a responsibility to stockholders, creditors, and employees that must be considered along with the responsibility to victims (Tyler, 1997). Simply put, there are times when an organization must protect its financial assets. Crisis managers choose what level of disclosure to employ during a crisis.

The disclosure debate raises the question of honesty. A common recommendation for crisis managers is to be honest. Honesty means not lying to stakeholders. Stakeholders are angrier when an organization lies about a crisis than when an organization has a crisis (Caruba, 1994). Limited disclosure is not meant to be a form of deception—not revealing critical information. In fact, an organization should fully disclose any and all information about a crisis if there are risks of further harm or even death resulting from the crisis. Limited disclosure should not be used as a form of stonewalling. It should be used to disclose only the information stakeholders need to know. Of course, what stakeholders need to know is difficult to define, and each crisis management team (CMT) should establish guidelines for when it will use full or limited disclosure (see Kaufmann et al., 1994; Tyler, 1997, for discussions about the ethics and procedures for using limited disclosure). Remember, lack of honesty seriously damages organization-stakeholder relationships—destroys the organization's reputation—and can lead to massive monetary awards against the organization in future lawsuits (Fitzpatrick, 1995).

Express Sympathy

Crises have the potential to create a entirely new class of stakeholders, the victims. Victims are those people who have suffered physically, mentally, or financially from the crisis. For instance, employees may be injured in an industrial accident, customers may be traumatized by the violence in an accident, or stockholders may lose dividends due to the costs of a recall or a drop in stock prices. The existence of victims affects the initial response. The spokesperson should express compassion for the victims during this first crisis statement (Augustine, 1995; Sen & Egelhoff, 1991). Expressing compassion does not mean an organization admits responsibility. Rather, the spokesperson expresses sympathy and concern for the victims. Sympathy can be expressed without incurring the liability associated with taking responsibility for a crisis (Fitzpatrick, 1995; Tyler, 1997). Compassion is linked to credibility as well. The compassion of an organization indicates that it is trustworthy—the organization is concerned about the needs of its stakeholders. Concern is an accepted part of trustworthiness (McCroskey, 1997).

Instructing Information

When a crisis hits, stakeholders want to know what happened and need to know how the crisis will or might affect them (Bergman, 1994; Trahan, 1993). Sturges (1994) refers to this as instructing information. There are three types of instructing information. First, there is the basic information about what happened or the what, when, where, why, and how information about the crisis (Ammerman, 1995; Bergman, 1994). Stakeholders are reassured when they know what happened. Second, stakeholders should be told if there is anything they themselves need to do to protect themselves from a crisis. Stakeholders may need to know to evacuate an area, boil drinking water, go somewhere for assistance, or return a defective product (Sturges, 1994). Third, stakeholders should be told what is being done to correct the problem. Stakeholders feel better when they know the crisis situation is being controlled. Instructing information furthers the perceptions that the organization has regained control of the situation. Knowing what happened, taking actions to help stakeholders, and taking steps to correct the situation all reflect an image of the organization being in control. The crisis team fosters the perception that the organization knows what is happening and is taking steps to eliminate the effects of the crisis (Birch, 1994).

The first priority in crisis communication is to deliver instructing information to stakeholders. Instructing information satisfies the needs of both the stakeholders and the crisis team. The stakeholders receive the information they require to protect themselves from the crisis. The crisis team cultivates the perception that the organization is once more in control of the situation. Once the instructing information has been presented, the crisis team can begin to use crisis communication to address reputational concerns.

The initial response is the first statement the spokesperson makes about the crisis. The value of the initial response in setting the tone for the remainder of the public aspect of the crisis management effort cannot be overstated. The initial statement serves to prevent the spread of misinformation and to build the credibility of the organization. When media reports are based on misinformation, the potential damage threat of the crisis intensifies for the organization (Barton, 1993). The crisis team needs to disseminate accurate crisis information as soon possible, even if that means reporting only the scant information that might be known currently about the crisis. The initial statement also builds the organization's credibility. The mere act of the response is symbolic because it indicates that the organization is regaining control of itself. Couple control with an expression of concern for the victims, and the organization has taken steps to improve both the expertise and trustworthiness dimensions of its credibility. Initial perceptions of credibility facilitate the crisis management process by making stakeholders more receptive to later messages.

APPLICATION POINT

Find an example of an actual initial crisis response. Use a recent case appearing in the news media, a favorite crisis of yours, or research one of the crises listed in the appendix. Evaluate the organization's initial response to the crisis. Use the five initial response recommendations presented in this chapter. What did the organization do well? What did it do poorly? How could it improve its performance?

Reputational Management Concerns

Reputational damage is a danger during any crisis. A number of crisis management experts have begun to explore how an organization's crisis communication strategies—what an organization says and does after a crisis hits—can be used to affect a reputation during a crisis. The belief is that communication (words and actions) does affect how stakeholders perceive the organization in crisis (Allen & Caillouet, 1994; Benoit, 1995, 1997; Hearit, 1994, 1996). The situation affects the selection of communication strategies. Therefore, the characteristics of a crisis situation will recommend the use of particular crisis communication strategies while ruling out the use of others (Benoit, 1995; Coombs, 1995a; Hobbs, 1995). Crisis managers can best protect an organizational reputation by understanding which crisis communication strategies work best in each type of crisis. An effective selection system is based on three points: (a) crisis managers must have a list of crisis communication strategies from which to choose, (b) crisis managers must have a system for categorizing crisis situations, and (c) the crisis managers must have some system for selecting the crisis communication strategies that best correspond to a particular crisis situation (Benson, 1988).

Crisis Communication Strategies

The crisis communication strategies represent the actual responses the organization uses to address the crisis. Communication has both verbal and nonverbal aspects. Hence, crisis communication strategies involve the words (verbal aspects) and actions (nonverbal aspects) the organization directs toward the crisis (Allen & Caillouet, 1994; Benoit, 1995). Crisis communication strategies were first examined as apologia or the use of communication to defend one's reputation from public attack (Ware & Linkugel, 1973). Because crises threaten a reputation, it was believed that organizations would use apologia strategies to defend their reputations (Dionisopolous & Vibbert, 1988). A number of crisis critics have applied the apologia strategies or stances to understand how organizations defend their reputations during a crisis (Hearit, 1994, 1996; Hobbs, 1995; Ice, 1991).

Apologia offered a rather limited number of crisis communication strategies. The belief was that strategies other than those found in apologia were being used in crisis responses. The number of crisis communication strategies was expanded by examining the concept of accounts. Accounts are statements people use to explain their behavior when that behavior is called into question. Crisis responses are a form of account. Similar to apologia, accounts involve protecting one's reputation from a threat (Benoit, 1995). Benoit (1995, 1997) has developed a list of 14 "image restoration strategies" based on apologia and account research. Allen and Caillouet (1994) used impression management and accounts to develop a list of 20 "impression management strategies" an organization might use. Impression management contends that communication can be used to strategically shape the public reputation of an organization. Organizations use the impression management strategies, what I term *crisis communication strategies,* to repair the reputational damage from a crisis.

Trying to specify the exact number of crisis communication strategies is a losing proposition (Benoit, 1995). A more productive approach is to identify the most common crisis communication strategies and discover a thread that connects them together. A list of seven common crisis communication strategies was derived by selecting those strategies that appeared on two or more lists developed by crisis experts. The seven crisis communication strategies are defined in Table 7.1.

A common thread for the crisis communication strategies is easy to find. Over the years, crisis researchers have created a variety of continuums for crisis communication strategies (e.g., Marcus & Goodman, 1991; Siomkos & Shrivastava, 1993). All the continuums reflect a range of actions from defensive to accommodative. Defensive strategies claim that there is no crisis or try to deny responsibility for the crisis. The emphasis is on protecting the organizational reputation, even at the expense of the victims. Accommodative strategies accept responsibility for or take remedial action to correct the crisis. The emphasis is on helping the victims, even if it hurts the organization's reputation or financial status (Marcus & Goodman, 1991; Siomkos &

TABLE 7.1 Crisis Communication Strategies Defined

Attack the accuser	Crisis manager confronts the person or group who claims that a crisis exists. The response may include a threat to use "force" (e.g., a lawsuit) against the accuser.
Denial	Crisis manager states that no crisis exists. The response may include explaining why there is no crisis.
Excuse	Crisis manager tries to minimize the organization's responsibility for the crisis. The response can include denying any intention to do harm or claiming the organization had no control of the events that led to the crisis.
Justification	Crisis manager tries to minimize the perceived damage associated with the crisis. The response can include stating there was no serious damage or injuries or claiming that the victims deserved what they received.
Ingratiation	Crisis manager praises a stakeholder or reminds stakeholders that the organization has done good deeds for them in the past.
Corrective action	Crisis managers seek to repair the damage from the crisis or take steps to prevent a repeat of the crisis.
Full apology	Crisis manager publicly states that the organization takes full responsibility for the crisis and asks forgiveness for the crisis. Some compensation (e.g., money or aid) may be included with the apology.

Shrivastava, 1993). The recurring theme indicates that crisis communication strategies should be arrayed along a continuum with end points of defensive and accommodative. Figure 7.1 places the common crisis communication strategies on just such a continuum.

Full apology is the most accommodative because it involves taking responsibility for the crisis and asking for forgiveness. The organization must acknowledge that it is responsible for the crisis. The organization then asks stakeholders to forgive its misstep. Some compensation (e.g., money or aid) can be included in the apology but is not necessary. Corrective action requires an organization to repair the damage created by the crisis or take action to prevent a repeat of the crisis. Sample correctives include cleaning up a chemical spill and instituting new inspection procedures to prevent another product defect. In each example, actions are being taken to help the victims, but the organization does not have to accept responsibility for the crisis.

Ingratiation is very near the middle of the continuum because it tries to offset the negatives of the crisis with positives. Stakeholders receive praise or are reminded of past good works performed by the organization. The organization does not deny the crisis, but neither does it accept responsibility. The organization tries to deal with stakeholder and reputational concerns simultaneously. Praising stakeholders recognizes their importance to the organization, whereas past good works show a history of concern for stake-

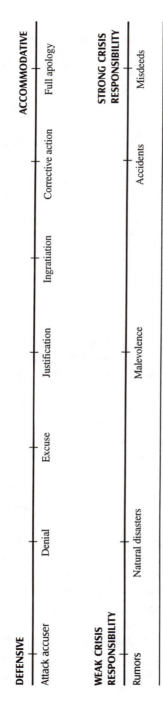

Figure 7.1. Matching Crises and Communication Strategies

124

holders. However, current stakeholder concerns about the crisis are not handled. Praising and bolstering try to establish organizational goodwill partly to protect the organization's image. The kind words and past good deeds inject positives into the negative crisis situation.

Justification accepts the crisis but tries to downplay the perceived severity of the crisis. Defining a crisis as minor trivializes victim concerns. By trying to reduce perceptions of severity, the organization is emphasizing the protection of the organizational reputation and downplaying the concerns of victims. Excuse acknowledges the crisis but works to reduce organizational responsibility for the crisis. Once more, the emphasis is on protecting the organizational reputation, not on concern for the victims. The organization uses lack of intent or lack of control to prove a lack of crisis responsibility. The concerns of the victims are not addressed because the organization denies any responsibility for them.

Denial states that there is no crisis or claims that the organization has no responsibility for the crisis. No crisis means there are no victims. No organizational responsibility implies that the organization has no connection to or responsibility for the victims. The organizational reputation is protected by denying the existence of victims or denying any responsibility for their problems. Attacking the accuser is the most defensive strategy because it goes beyond denial to attacking some stakeholder group. The organization is attacking stakeholders that claim a crisis and victims exist. An example would be an organization suing an environmental group that is blocking a construction project. The lawsuit is an attack. The organization denies the concerns of the stakeholders while charging them with wrongdoing. The accommodative-defensive continuum will be an important resource when trying to match crisis communication strategies with crisis situations.

Crisis Situations

When developing the crisis portfolio described in Chapter 5, it was noted that crises can be grouped into types. These types can be further grouped into families, an important step in the development of the crisis communication strategy selection process. The selection of crisis communication strategies is based in part on the characteristics of the crisis situation. Some system of categorizing crises is necessary to begin the matching process. The key is to develop a categorization system that can be tied to the accommodative-defensive response continuum. Without a connection to the crisis communication strategies, the crisis category system has little value.

A natural link between crisis communication strategies and crisis situations is crisis responsibility. Crisis responsibility is the degree to which stakeholders feel the organization is responsible for the crisis (Coombs & Holladay, 1996). As the reputational damage of a crisis intensifies, perceptions of crisis responsibility strengthen along with the need for more accommodative strategies (Coombs, 1998). When perceptions of crisis responsibility are strong, the crisis managers must address the needs of victims, take responsibility, and/or rectify the situation—be accommodative. Defensive strategies such as denial or justification become less effective because the organization is perceived as responsible for the crisis (Benoit, 1995). Thus, categorizing crisis situations by crisis responsibility provides a means of matching crisis situations to crisis communication strategies.

The CMP discussion in Chapter 5 identified nine basic crises: natural disasters, malevolence, technical breakdowns, human breakdowns, confrontation, megadamage, organizational misdeeds, rumors, and workplace violence (see Chapter 5 for the definitions of each crisis). Research has shown that these nine can be grouped into five families when organizational responsibility is used as the sorting mechanism (Coombs et al., 1995; Mitroff, 1988; Pauchant & Mitroff, 1992). The five groups are rumors, natural disasters, malevolence, accidents (technical breakdowns, challenges, workplace violence, and megadamage), and misdeeds (organizational misdeeds and human breakdowns).

Figure 7.1 also arrays the crises along a continuum from strong to weak crisis responsibility. Misdeeds top the list with the strongest perceptions of organizational responsibility. This is to be expected because misdeeds involve organizational members taking actions that they know are wrong (i.e., violate sexual harassment regulations) or place stakeholders at risk (i.e., letting a potentially dangerous product remain on the market). Stakeholders believe misdeeds should be prevented by the organization.

Accidents have the next strongest perceptions of organizational responsibility. Although unintentional, accidents are considered to be preventable to some degree (Tyler, 1997). Stakeholders have become less likely to believe that industrial accidents are not preventable. Accidents seem to be linked to irresponsible corporate action rather than chance (Heath, 1994). For instance, perhaps improved safety procedures could have prevented the industrial accident. Zilog's semiconductor factory in Idaho testifies to the ability to improve safety. Over a period of 3 years, Zilog spent $10 million to reduce the extremely high accident rate at the facility. Its injury rate from accidents went from well above to below the industry average during the 3-year stretch (Smith, 1998). Although an organization always has room for improving accident reduction, lack of intention to do harm helps to create perceptions of minimal organizational responsibility.

Rumors, malevolence, and natural disasters are at the low end of the organizational responsibility continuum. There is nothing an organization can due to prevent natural disasters; hence, it generates very weak perceptions of organizational control. Rumors are untruths, so there is no real crisis if stakeholders reject the rumors. Malevolence also produces rather weak perceptions of organizational control. Stakeholders view malevolence as fate; if someone wants to harm an organization, he or she will do so. Still, organizations are expected to take steps to prevent tampering. Although organizations can take precautions against malevolence, it cannot stop evildoers completely. For instance, Johnson & Johnson instituted triple safety-sealed, tamper-resistant packaging after the 1982 Tylenol capsule poisonings. The packaging was hailed as a fantastic safety measure and helped to restore consumer confidence in Tylenol capsules. On February 8, 1986, a New York woman died from poisoned Tylenol capsules she bought at the A&P. Once more, the evidence pointed to product tampering rather than a production error ("Headache," 1986). The new packaging could not protect consumers completely. Even more so than for accidents, malevolence is considered a fact of life that organizations can do little to prevent (Coombs, 1998; Coombs & Holladay, 1996).

Communication is a concern throughout the entire crisis management process. Crisis managers rely on communication before, during, and after a crisis. Crisis communication strategies are just one aspect of communication's ubiquitous role in crisis management.

Crisis Communication Strategy Selection

One guide for crisis communication strategy selection is to move more toward accommodative strategies as perceptions of crisis responsibility intensify. Figure 7.1 visually depicts the matching system. Organizational misdeeds require crisis managers to use accommodative strategies. A full apology with corrective action is recommended to maximize concern for victims. However, liability concerns may limit the ability of the organization to take responsibility. Still, an organization can express concern without opening itself up to liability damages (Fitzpatrick, 1995; Tyler, 1997). In accidents, crisis managers can use a mix of excuse, justification, ingratiation, and corrective action—the middle of the continuum. Crisis managers have a greater latitude of action when organizational responsibility is minimal (Sen & Egelhoff, 1991). Accidents are unintentional, so excuse is appropriate, and corrective actions help to show concern for victims. Remember, it is commonly recommended to demonstrate compassion for victims. A negative reputation based on past crises or poor performance can restrict the crisis manager's options in an accident. A history of the same or similar accidents leads people to believe that the current crisis could have been avoided. The repetition indicates that the fault lies with the organization and is not a random occurrence. When an organization has a negative reputation, corrective action is necessary because stakeholders are less likely to believe that an accident was unpreventable (Heath, 1994).

Natural disasters allow crisis managers to use the excuse strategy. The spokesperson reinforces that the crisis is not the organization's fault. Malevolence permits crisis managers to employ the excuse and the corrective action. Because malevolence is associated with very little organizational responsibility, an excuse works fine. However, stakeholders like to know that additional precautions are being taken to prevent a repeat, so a corrective strategy is recommended as well (Benoit, 1995). Rumors require crisis managers to use the denial or attack accuser strategies. Denial is used when there is no clear accuser. Attack-the-accuser works when the crisis offers a clear accuser who is providing inaccurate information (Fearn-Banks, 1996). The use of justification and ingratiation is a function of the crisis and the organization. Ingratiation can be used during any crisis if the organization has a strong reputation—a history of good works (Coombs, 1995a). Justification can be used in accidents, malevolence, and natural disasters if the damage is truly minimal. Table 7.2 summarizes the recommendations for crisis communication strategy selection.

The crisis communication strategies are what Sturges (1994) calls internalizing information. Internalizing information is used by stakeholders to help form their perceptions of the organizational reputation. As such, the crisis communication strategies should not be used until after the instructing information has been communicated to stakeholders (Sturges, 1994). Jumping right to reputational management makes the organization look self-serving. The information needs of the stakeholders must be met prior to the use of reputational management efforts.

APPLICATION POINT

Crisis managers try to protect the organization's reputation during a crisis. This chapter presents some guidelines for selecting crisis

TABLE 7.2 Crisis Communication Strategy Selection Summary

Full apology	Used when the crisis is the result of an organizational misdeed.
Corrective action	Used when the crisis is an organizational misdeed and is recommended for accidents too. Accidents involving an organization with a history of crises should use corrective actions along with other strategies.
Ingratiation	Used only if the organization has a strong reputation—a history of good works. It is appropriate for any type of crisis.
Justification	Used only when the crisis damage is minimal. It is appropriate for accidents, malevolence, and natural disasters.
Excuse	Used when an organization has little responsibility for the crisis. It is appropriate for accidents, malevolence, or natural disasters. It is unwise to employ the strategy when crisis damage is severe; it makes the organization look petty, especially for accidents.
Denial	Used when there is evidence that no crisis exists or that the organization is not responsible for the crisis. It is appropriate for rumors or challenge crises.
Attack the accuser	Used when there is an identifiable and refutable attacker. It is appropriate for rumors or challenge crises.

response strategies to protect the reputation. Now is your chance to apply the guidelines. Two different cases are offered as practice exercises.

▓ Case 1: The Challenge

You are on the CMT of a large chain of bookstores in the United States. A conservative organization called Americans for Family Values (AFV) condemns your chain for being one of the largest pornography distributors in the United States. AFV announces it will boycott your chain and picket select stores if your company does not stop selling Penthouse, Playboy, and certain offensive books, including fine photography books that used nude models. AFV claims a membership of more than 500,000 people. Three years ago, AFV used a similar strategy to get a large convenience store chain to stop selling Penthouse and Playboy. The news media are interested in the story. Given the situation, what crisis response strategy or strategies would you use to best protect your company's reputation? Why do think your selections will be effective?

Case 2: Odometer Incident

You are on the CMT of a U.S. automobile manufacturer. Each year your company road tests 2% of the cars and trucks it builds. The road tests are used as a quality check. The drives are usually less than 40 miles but are very hard miles on the vehicle. The road-tested vehicles are then sold as new to customers. From 1992 to 1994, two executives ordered that odometers be disconnected during road tests. Customers who bought the vehicles during the 2-year time span never knew their vehicles had been road tested. No laws were broken, but a class action lawsuit has been filed against your company, and your two executives are under government investigation. Given the situation, what crisis response strategy or strategies would you use to best protect your company's reputation? Why do believe your selections will be effective?

Communicating the Contingency Plan

As noted in the crisis management plan, stakeholders must be made aware of the enactment of the contingency or business resumption plan. The contingency plan outlines what the organization will do to maintain operations and restore business as usual. Various stakeholders need to be informed about the implementation of your contingency plan. For example, maintaining operations may involve renting equipment, using different facilities, and even hiring other employees. This phase is known as interim processing (Myers, 1993). All the people and vendors necessary to get the interim processing phase up and running must be contacted and given specific instructions. Moreover, employees, suppliers, and distributors must know how the interim processing will affect them. Once business is restored to normal, the relevant stakeholders must be informed of the change as well (Myers, 1993). The crisis management plan should specify arrangements for identifying the relevant stakeholders for the contingency plan and for communicating with these stakeholders.

Follow-Up Communication

With all the emphasis on the initial response, it is easy to overlook follow-up communication with stakeholders. Crisis communication should continue throughout the life cycle of the crisis. Spokespersons must stay in touch with stakeholders. Although the initial response has a mass media emphasis, follow-up communication can be better targeted to individual stakeholders. Better targeting means using the channels best suited to reaching the stakeholder and tailoring the message to fit the needs of the stakeholder (Carney & Jorden, 1993; Clampitt, 1991; Fombrun & Shanley, 1990). For instance, major stockholders may learn about the crisis from the news media. Follow-up communication to stockholders would center on the financial implications of the crisis—their primary concern—and use either calls or specially printed updates from the investor relations department. The stakeholder communication network is valuable at this point. As noted in Chapter 5, the stakeholder information network will have the necessary contact information and preferred channels for reaching the stakeholders.

In addition to answering new inquires, follow-up communication involves delivering the promised information and updating the stakeholders about new developments. As noted earlier, there are times when crisis managers do not have answers to stakeholder questions. To avoid silence and "no comment" responses, the spokespersons are recommended to explain that they do not have the information necessary to answer the questions at this time but will pass the information along as soon as they receive it (Stewart & Cash, 1997). Such a response is a promise by the crisis team. It is essential that the crisis team fulfills these promises. The crisis team must report to the stakeholders, even if it is only to say that the information was never found. Credibility and the organizational reputation are built on organizations matching words and deeds (Herbig et al., 1994). The crisis managers' words include their promises, but their actions fulfill their promises. An organization loses credibility and damages the organization-stakeholder relationships when crisis managers fail to deliver on their information promises.

Updates inform stakeholders about the progress of the crisis management effort. Four pieces of information are crucial to updates. First, let stakeholders know how the recovery effort is progressing. Second, announce the cause of the crisis as soon as it is known if the cause was not known at the time of the initial message. Third, inform stakeholders of any actions taken to prevent a repeat of the crisis, including when those changes have been implemented. Fourth, report to stakeholders any third-party support your organization is receiving. Third-party support means that outside groups are praising your crisis management efforts or agreeing with your assessment of the situation. Examples include noted crisis experts giving the crisis management effort a positive review in the news media or the government saying that the organization's stated cause of the crisis is correct. Supplying these four kinds of information builds the credibility of the organization. Pieces one, two, and three reinforce a perception of control, and piece four provides added credibility with the endorsement of an outside expert.

Two final points about follow-up communication must be made. First, the spokespersons should continue to field and respond to inquires throughout the crisis. The crisis team must track and answer all inquires. Second, the spokesperson should continue to express compassion in the follow-up communication. Losing sight of the victims in later messages can call the initial concern into question. Was the organization simply posturing in the news media? The organizational compassion must be real and be reflected in the follow-up communication. Follow-up includes both words and actions (Bergman, 1994; Mitchell, 1986). If aid is promised to victims, make sure it appears. Once more, tracking crisis information is critical. The crisis team should be recording what follow-up actions were promised on the stakeholder relations worksheets. Again, credibility is based on the organization's words matching its actions.

APPLICATION POINT

Crisis managers must know what points need follow-up if follow-up is to be effective. The next two cases place you in the position of deciding what follow-up is necessary in the crisis situation.

Case 1: The Oil Spill

On January 2, 1988, a four million-gallon storage tank ruptured while being filled. The tank belonged to the Ashland Oil Company. Millions of gallons of fuel poured into the Monongehela River and headed toward the Ohio River. The Monongehela is a tributary of the Ohio. In all, the oil spill disrupted the water supply of 850,000 people. Cities could not draw water from the two rivers for purification until the spill had dissipated. Ashland immediately notified government agencies and hired experienced cleanup crews. Ashland worked to restore water in many communities and provided more than 15 million gallons of water by truck and barge. Ashland management accepted full financial responsibility for the spill and apologized to those affected. For instance, in one community, displaced residents were reimbursed all expenses, given

$200 for inconveniences, and received a written apology from Ashland management. Actions were taken to settle all lawsuits quickly and fairly. The media and crisis experts praised Ashland for its response. As a member of the Ashland CMT, what follow-up actions might be needed? Be sure to list the stakeholders requiring follow-up, why they would need follow-up, and what channels you would use to reach each stakeholder.

▨ Case 2: The Product Recall

Martin Feeds, Inc. makes a variety of animal feeds. A few years ago, trace amounts of monensin, a poultry medicine, were discovered in a batch of dog food. Monensin is toxic for dogs. Martin Feeds examined the dog food after reports that some dogs had become ill after eating its food. Initial reports indicated that no dogs had died from the poisoning. Martin Feeds voluntarily recalled 1,200 bags of dog food. It also worked to settle all claims and pay veterinary costs quickly. The final cost of the settlements and recall was $500,000. As a member of the Martin Feeds CMT, what follow-up actions might be needed? Be sure to list the stakeholders requiring follow-up, why they would need follow-up, and what channels you would use to reach each stakeholder.

Conclusion

The actions taken in the crisis containment and recovery phase are informed by the crisis-related information gathered during the crisis recognition phase. The crisis team seeks to contain the damage and return to business as usual as soon as possible. Communication is essential to shortening the duration of the crisis because it is at the heart of the initial response, strengthening reputational management, informing stakeholders, and providing follow-up information. The initial response allows the crisis team to reestablish a sense of organizational control over events and express compassion for victims. Taking early control of the crisis prevents rumors and speculation from needlessly intensifying the crisis damage. Moreover, the response must be quick and consistent while the organization remains open to communication with stakeholders. A favorable organization-stakeholder relationship facilitates the initial response.

Crisis communication is ideal for combating the reputational damage associated with a crisis. Crisis communication strategies affect how stakeholders perceive the crisis and the organization in crisis. In addition, the crisis itself limits the type of crisis communication strategies that can be used effectively. Crisis managers should select the crisis communication strategies that fit best with their particular crisis situation. The contingency plan allows an organization to function during a crisis and return to business as usual more quickly. Crisis managers must communicate to relevant stakeholders how the contingency plan affects their interaction with the organization. In addition to the initial response, crisis managers have a variety of follow-up information that they must communicate to stakeholders. The follow-up information includes delivery of previously promised information and updates regarding the progress of the crisis management efforts. The ongoing organization-stakeholder dialogue continues throughout the crisis management process.

Regular two-way communication between the organization and the stakeholders (a dialogue) is the lifeblood of a favorable organization-stakeholder relationship. The dialogue must be maintained during good and bad times. Crises are part of the bad times. Remembering the importance of communicating with stakeholders aids the CMT in its efforts to contain and recover from the crisis.

8

Postcrisis Concerns

E ventually, all crises come to an end. The end means that the immediate effects of the crisis are past, and the organization returns to business as usual. Crisis managers should not feel that their work is completed when the crisis ends. First, it is critical that crisis managers evaluate their efforts. Organizations learn to improve the crisis management efforts through evaluation. Second, crises are still monitored after they are resolved. Monitoring might involve cooperating in any continuing investigations or supplying necessary updated information to stakeholders.

This chapter begins by examining the role of evaluation in crisis management learning. The evaluation efforts link back to earlier crisis management steps, thus reflecting the ongoing nature of crisis management. Evaluation is the key to improvement in crisis management. One way to improve the crisis management process is by learning what the organization did right or wrong during the crisis management effort. Evaluation yields insights into the crisis management effort, which should be treated as crisis management lessons. Because lessons should be remembered, the idea of institutional memory is discussed after evaluation. The chapter ends by reviewing the follow-up activities a crisis manager may need to perform and how the postcrisis actions naturally lead back to crisis preparation.

Crisis Evaluation

An actual crisis is a "tremendous opportunity for learning" (Pauchant & Mitroff, 1992, p. 158). Learning is accomplished through evaluation of the crisis management efforts. Crisis managers use evaluation in two distinct ways. First, how the organization dealt with the crisis—crisis management performance—is evaluated. Crisis management performance evaluation involves examining the efficacy of the crisis management plan (CMP) and the execution of the CMP (Barton, 1993; Newsom et al., 1996). The crisis team carefully examines all phases of crisis management performance. Second, crisis impact is evaluated. Crisis impact evaluation includes a review of the actual damage created by the crisis (Sen & Egelhoff, 1991). A natural link exists between the two forms of evaluation. The actual crisis damage should be less than the anticipated crisis damage if the crisis management efforts were effective. Thus, damage assessments provide a tangible indicator of crisis management success or failure.

Crisis Management Performance Evaluation

Crisis management performance is primarily a function of the quality of the CMP and the crisis team's ability to make it work. Failure could result from an ineffectual CMP, poor execution of the CMP, or both (Mitroff et al., 1996; Newsom et al., 1996). An organization must understand the source of failure or success if it is to learn from either. What lessons are learned if the organization does not know what it did right or wrong? Moreover, certain structural (i.e., technology and infrastructure) features can facilitate or inhibit crisis performance (Mitroff et al., 1996). All facets of the crisis management performance must be evaluated to determine its true strengths and weaknesses.

Data Collection

Data collection is the first step in any evaluation process. Evaluation data come from the crisis records, stakeholder feedback, and media coverage. The various crisis records serve to document vital information such as the notification process, the collection and processing of information, the reception and answering of stakeholder queries, the crisis-related messages sent by the organization, and significant decisions and actions taken by the crisis management team (CMT). The primary sources of crisis documentation are the incident report sheets, the CMT strategy worksheets, the stakeholder contact worksheets, and the information log sheet. The crisis records should be reviewed to determine if there were any noticeable mistakes made by the

CMT. For example, was important information not processed, were stakeholder queries ignored, or were inappropriate messages sent to stakeholders?

All stakeholder groups involved in the crisis should be asked for feedback, including employees and external stakeholders. The feedback can be collected by structured surveys, interviews, or focus groups. Simple surveys seem to be the most effective method. Surveys minimize the time demands placed on the stakeholders and ensure that the evaluators are receiving the information they want. Typical questions on a crisis evaluation survey include the person's role in the crisis, satisfaction with and ways to improve notification, comments on specific strengths or weaknesses in the crisis management performance, and suggestions for improving the CMP (Barton, 1993). Different evaluation forms are required for the crisis team members, employees, and external stakeholders. The three groups have different connections to the crisis management process. Obviously, it is more difficult to get the cooperation of external stakeholders, but every effort must be made to gather data that will provide a holistic picture of the crisis management performance. Media coverage is another type of stakeholder feedback. The CMT should collect all media reports about the crisis. The CMT may choose to hire an independent consulting firm to collect the crisis performance data.

Organizing and Analyzing the
Crisis Management Performance Data

Once collected, the data must be organized for the analysis. A danger in evaluation is making too general of an analysis. For crisis management, a basic overall good or poor performance evaluation would be too general. Specificity is the key to useful evaluation. Specify in detail what was done well and done poorly. The specifics tell organizational evaluators what changes need to be made and what must be retained. Mitroff et al. (1996) provided a number of helpful suggestions for organizing and analyzing the crisis evaluation data. Mitroff et al. suggested organizing the crisis evaluation data using four major crisis variables: crisis type, crisis phases, systems, and stakeholders. The four variables divide the evaluation data into small, discernible units. The crisis managers can target strengths and weaknesses more precisely when data are divided, a form of data splitting. The value of Mitroff et al.'s approach becomes clearer when the application of the specific crisis variables is considered.

Organizations face many different types of crises. Crisis teams may not handle all crises equally well. Crisis managers will want to compare evaluations from different crisis types to ascertain if patterns of strengths and weaknesses are crisis specific (Mitroff et al., 1996; Pearson & Mitroff, 1993). Categorizing evaluations by crisis type permits cross-crisis comparisons. Comparing crisis performance across crisis types is one form of analysis.

A basic premise of this book is that crises move through distinct phases. Crisis management has been organized around three phases, with each having three subphases. Crisis teams may handle the phases and subphases with different degrees of success and failure. For instance, the crisis team may be adept at finding information but have problems articulating the organizational crisis response. Dividing the crisis evaluation data by crisis phases and subphases can help you identify if the crisis team or CMP is weak in a particular phase or subphase. The crisis team could work on the skills associated with the specific phase or subphase, and the CMP could be revised to improve preparation for that phase or subphase. Only by dividing evaluation data according to phases and subphases can the analysis reveal these types of specific strengths and weaknesses.

Systems include technology, human factors, infrastructure, culture, and emotions or beliefs. Technical systems organize the company work. Technical systems would include specific tasks along with the tools and materials necessary to complete them. Evaluators might ask, "Was the CMT hampered by lack of technical system support for crisis management?" The human factor system is the integration of people and machinery. It examines the fit between people and technology. Evaluators might ask, "Were the crisis management problems a function of a poor match between people and technology?" Infrastructure refers to the connection of the CMT to the functioning of the organization. A permanent CMT should exist and be integrated into the operation of the organization. Evaluators might ask, "Did the CMT fail because it is not considered a functioning part of the organization?" The cultural system refers to the extent to which the organization is oriented toward crisis preparation. Evaluators might ask, "Were the problems a function of cultural constraints such as suppressing bad news?" Finally, the emotional or belief system represents the dominant coalition's mind-set about crisis management. Evaluators might ask, "Did the crisis management effort fail because the dominant coalition does not support crisis preparation or the crisis response?" The examination of system-specific concerns helps to determine if the crisis management performance might have been a function of structural factors rather than the CMP or the CMT (Mitroff et al., 1996).

The system variables reflect the ongoing nature of crisis management as well. The evaluation of system variables is most appropriate during the preparation phase. An organization can and should identify system flaws before a crisis hits. However, sometimes the flaws are hidden and do not surface until an actual crisis occurs. For example, the dominant coalition may espouse support for crisis management until there is a crisis. Then their support may evaporate. Or the stress of the crisis management process creates unexpected problems in how people use technology.

Reactions from all stakeholders affected by the particular crisis are needed for a thorough evaluation. How did they feel about the crisis management performance? The only way to assess stakeholder reactions is to ask them. A cardinal rule in evaluation is to not assume that you know how people feel about a message or action. By considering each stakeholder separately, an organization can determine specific strengths and weaknesses. The evaluators can determine which actions were effective or ineffective for specific stakeholder groups. For example, stockholders might be happy with the type of information and how they received it, but the community may be disappointed with how they received their crisis-related information. Specific stakeholder reactions also will indicate which parts of the stakeholder network are effective or ineffective during crisis management.

However the data are divided, the key is to find the specific strengths and weaknesses of the CMP, the CMT, and structural features of the organization. Evaluations that are too general serve little purpose if the goal is to improve crisis management performance. The CMP should be revised by noting the strengths and developing ways to correct the weaknesses. Crisis team members must be evaluated for both individual-level and group-level factors. As noted in Chapter 5, certain knowledge, skills, and traits are helpful in a crisis team member. In addition, the crisis team must perform as a group. Thus, the group-level factors such as group decision making are relevant during evaluation. The crisis management evaluation data should yield assessments of how individual team members performed as well as how the team as a whole performed.

Impact Evaluation

The crisis management performance should help the organization by protecting it from damage in some way. Crisis management is designed to protect important organizational assets such as people, reputation, and financial concerns (Barton, 1993; Marcus & Goodman, 1991). The crisis management performance evaluation should include measures of damage factors that reflect success or failure in protecting assets. The damage factors include financial, reputational, human, secondary financial, media frames, and media coverage duration. The financial factors are fairly standard: earnings per share, stock prices, sales, and market share (Baucus & Baucus, 1997; Baucus & Near, 1991; Sen & Egelhoff, 1991).

The reputational factors involve perceptions of the organization. Three related elements are relevant to assessing a crisis reputation: the pre- and postcrisis reputation scores, media coverage of the crisis, and stakeholder feedback. Any organization that expends resources on managing its reputation should bother to track its reputation over time. The organization should assess its reputation on a regular basis—solicit evaluations of its reputation from stakeholders. Comparing pre- and postcrisis organizational reputations is the strongest indicator of the reputational impact of a crisis.

Reputations are built from stakeholder experiences with the organization. During a crisis, stakeholders experience an organization through the media and its crisis management actions. The media portrayals of the organization and the crisis can be critical in shaping the perceptions of other stakeholders involved in the crisis (Fearn-Banks, 1996; Pearson & Clair, 1998). Stories of an uncaring organization in disarray erode a reputation and injure the stakeholder-organization relationship. The media's power intensifies when it is the primary channel for reaching stakeholders. The media stories become the only crisis experiences when stakeholders have no other contact with the organization—in other words, are media dependent. Experts believe that stakeholder crisis evaluations will reflect the media depictions. Thus, if the media are critical of the organization, its reputation with stakeholders could suffer. Conversely, the reputation would be protected by favorable media portrayals (Nelkin, 1988).

Organizations should use standard publicity analysis techniques to evaluate crisis coverage. Analysts examine the media stories for positive and negative statements about the organization. To preserve important details, the positive and negative statements should be grouped by subphase. Grouping by subphase will indicate precisely where the crisis managers were perceived as doing something good or bad.

Media coverage is an imprecise substitute for actual reputational measures. Stakeholders do not always absorb and parrot the media's opinions. Stakeholders may disagree with the media reports, especially if the reports run counter to their perceptions of the organization. As Chapter 4 details, a strong reputation is hard to change because people reject contrary information about the reputation. The media are not all powerful.

Skilled crisis managers communicate to stakeholders through channels other than the news media. A well-developed stakeholder network provides the foundation for more direct contact with stakeholders. Thus, assessments of stakeholder satisfaction with the crisis management performance are critical. As noted previously, external feedback from stakeholders should be part of any crisis management performance evaluation. Negative feedback suggests that there will be reputational damage because stakeholders perceive the crisis was mishandled. Conversely, positive feedback indicates that the CMT's good work should protect the reputation. Stakeholder evaluations have limitations when used to evaluate reputations; they are an imprecise substitute for actual reputation measures. As with the media coverage, other factors are at work. Media analysis and stakeholder feedback provide crude reputational indices but are useful when direct measures of reputation are lacking.

Human factors focus on victims, including deaths, injuries, disruptions (e.g., evacuations or changes in daily routines caused by the crisis), and environmental damage. Injuries, death, and disruptions can be recorded in total numbers and severity for injuries and disruptions. Environmental damage is included with human factors because injuries and death are often associated with it, even though we are talking about animals and plants in this case. Perhaps crisis management has no more noble goal than to protect the human factors. Secondary financial factors are a reminder of the crisis because they continue to drain financial resources. Secondary financial factors include lawsuits (number and total value) and new regulations. A large number of and/or expensive lawsuits drain an organization's financial resources. Court costs are a burden to any financial settlements. The litigation costs help to explain why some organizations settle lawsuits while professing innocence and stating that the settlement was necessary to end the costly litigation process. MetPath, Inc., a leading medical testing laboratory, paid $35 million to settle fraud charges while maintaining it did nothing wrong. The new regulations are actions the government takes in response to a crisis. For example, the government may enact regulations to prevent a repeat of the crisis. The U.S. government considered banning the use of capsules for over-the-counter medications after the Sudafed and second Tylenol tamperings. Compliance with new regulations can create a financial impact that lasts for years (Sen & Egelhoff, 1991).

Media frames refer to the success of placing the organization's side of the story in the media. The organization's side of the story involves accurate information about what happened in the crisis and the organization's response—the organization's interpretation of the crisis. Analysts search for evidence markers of their side of the story in the media reports. Evidence markers include quotations from organizational spokespersons, media use of organizational sound bites, and accurate descriptions of the crisis event. Media frame success is measured two ways. First is a comparison of the amount of organizational frame material verses counterframe materials in the media coverage. For instance, who was quoted more by the media, the organization or its critics? Second is the accuracy of the crisis-related information appearing in the media. The higher the percentage of information the organization considers to be accurate, the more successful its media frame efforts.

The duration of the crisis' media coverage is the final evaluative point. Effective crisis management tries to move a crisis out of the media (Higbee, 1992). A crisis moves out of the media by becoming uninteresting to the media—it loses its newsworthiness. Effective crisis management seeks to inform stakeholders and bring closure to a crisis. Both actions reduce newsworthiness. The information vacuum created by a crisis makes it newsworthy. The audience interest in news value is at work. Once stakeholders have the facts, particularly the cause of the crisis, audience curiosity and interest fade. When actions indicate that a crisis is over, such as repaired damage or a return to normal operations, the situation loses the news value of being unusual. Conversely, crisis management errors, such as instigating conflict, prolong media coverage by sustaining the newsworthiness of a crisis. Two cases will illustrate the relationship between newsworthiness and media coverage.

In May 1985, E. F. Hutton officials pleaded guilt to 2,000 counts of wire and mail fraud and paid a $2 million fine. The story attracted mild media attention as people wondered what had happened at this high-profile investment firm. In September 1985, E. F. Hutton officials announced the results of former Attorney General Griffin Bell's investigation of the case. Bell had been hired by E. F. Hutton to find the cause of the crisis and to provide corrective measures. E. F. Hutton fired 14 executives criticized in the report and pledged to institute other reforms designed to prevent a repeat of the crisis (Koepp, 1985). The media quickly lost interest after the report was issued. Penalties had been paid, guilt admitted, the "why" question answered, and E. F. Hutton was working to prevent a repeat of the crisis. The crisis appeared resolved, stripping it of any newsworthiness.

In April 1996, the Equal Employment Opportunity Commission (EEOC) filed a major sexual harassment lawsuit against Mitsubishi Motor Manufacturing of America. Mitsubishi denied the charges and began a series or attacks against the EEOC. The response was deemed hostile by many observers and was highlighted by a media event when about 2,900 Mitsubishi workers demonstrated at EEOC offices in Chicago. Technically, the protest was organized by workers. However, Mitsubishi played a major role in facilitating the demonstration by allowing time off and helping to arrange bus transportation to Chicago (Annen & McCormick, 1997). The verbal barbs were aimed at the EEOC, and the litigation continued through 1997, as did the negative media coverage. When Mitsubishi's consultant, former Labor Secretary Lynn Martin, released a report on improving the workplace, the media greeted the announcement with skepticism, and the crisis remained alive. The Mitsubishi-EEOC conflict kept the story alive by making it newsworthy. Crisis managers should try to reduce, not increase, the newsworthiness of a crisis. A CMT has erred when its actions prolong media coverage of the crisis.

An assessment of the financial, reputational, human, secondary financial, media frame, and media duration factors enable you to measure the final impact of the crisis. But how does this help with the evaluation of crisis management performance? Alone, these factors do not evaluate crisis performance. They simply describe the impact of the crisis. What crisis managers must do is compare the outcome to (a) the projections made if no actions were taken to manage the crisis and (b) the desired objectives of the CMT. Although speculation is involved in both cases, careful projections can be made. Similar procedures are used in evaluating issues management efforts (Jones & Chase, 1979). Honesty is important; the CMT must not inflate the potential damage or low-ball its objectives if the exercise is to be a meaningful. What the damage assessment provides is some "objective" verification that the effect of the crisis performance was positive, negative, or of no consequence to the organization.

APPLICATION POINT

Find an example of an actual crisis response. Use a recent case appearing in the news media, a favorite crisis of yours, or research one of the crises listed in the appendix. Conduct an impact evaluation using as many of the damage factors discussed in this chapter. According to your analysis, how did the CMT perform during the crisis?

Evaluation Summary

All of the various crisis performance data and analyses should be condensed into a final report, complete with an executive summary and recommendations. Remember, the purposes are learning and improving crisis performance, not placing blame. Once completed, the evaluation indicates (a) if the CMT did what it should have done and did so effectively, (b) if the CMP proved useful in anticipating and resolving situations created by the crisis, (c) if structural features facilitated or hindered the crisis management effort, and (d) if the evaluation provides an assessment of the crisis damage. Combined, this evaluation will identify specific strengths and weaknesses of the CMT, the CMP, and the organization. Furthermore, the inclusion of damage analyses indicates if a crisis management performance is deemed good and actually protected the organization from damage. Sometimes a crisis team can execute a CMP well but still face massive damage, or a team can perform a suspect plan poorly yet the organization suffers little damage. For example, Johnson & Johnson had no CMP when if successfully handled the 1982 Tylenol tampering. There are exceptions to all rules, but crisis managers should not count on luck. Crisis managers prepare for crises so that they do not have to depend on luck.

Institutional Memory

Analysis creates crisis lessons. What use are crisis lessons if they cannot be recalled to help prevent a repeat of a mistake or to re-create a success? Remembering and recall are the domains of institutional memory (Pearson & Mitroff, 1993). Like people, organizations can store information for later use (Weick, 1979). A crisis should not be wasted. "Direct experience with a crisis, although painful, teaches more than even the best scenario ever could" (Newsom et al., 1996, p. 544). Evaluation reveals the lessons that hard experience teaches to the organization. The crisis lessons must be remembered by becoming a part of institutional memory.

Effective institutional memory involves storage and retrieval (Weick, 1979). First, there must be some means of recording and storing the crisis information—the crisis documentation and the evaluation report and crisis lessons. Sample storage options include hard copies and/or computer files. Either means requires redundancy and storage at multiple locations (Pauchant & Mitroff, 1992). Not all crisis information is of the same quality. Some information is more accurate (more fact than speculation) and more comprehensive (is more complete and contains fewer potential errors) (Garvin, 1996). Storage is more than recording information; it also involves rating the quality of the information. Key crisis information should be rated for accuracy and comprehensiveness when it is stored. The intranet is a logical place to store crisis information for easy retrieval.

To be of use later, the crisis information must be easy to retrieve. Retrieval involves being able to search and locate specific details (Weick, 1979). Intranet systems can have their own search mechanisms. Careful organization and input of the crisis information will permit easy searches and retrieval during later crisis management efforts. Once more we see that recording is not a simple process. The crisis information must be carefully and accurately stored if it is to be useful during later crisis management efforts. Each organization must develop its own system for organizing crisis information into a format that is searchable and retrievable.

Institutional memory requires one word of warning—do not become a slave to memory (Weick, 1979). Crisis managers must be willing to disregard past actions and information if they do not fit well with the current crisis. Blindly following past successes can lead to blunders when the past crisis is not wholly consistent with the current crisis. Institutional memory of crises can help to create an information acquisition bias. Assuming that a new crisis is just like an old crisis leads the crisis team to ignore information signaling that the new crisis differs in important ways. The institutional memory of past crises is both a blessing and a curse. However, the skilled CMT should be able to overcome the blind spot of information acquisition bias.

Postcrisis Actions

The responsibility of the crisis team continues until all crisis-related obligations are fulfilled. The postcrisis tasks can be divided into three groups: follow-up communication, cooperation with investigations, and crisis tracking. Even though the organization is back to normal operations and the immediate effects dissipate, the cause of the crisis may still be under investigation by government officials. The crisis team must be sure it cooperates with any investigation. Cooperation builds goodwill with the government agencies involved and indicates to other stakeholders that the organization is open and honest. Openness leads to the topic of follow-up communication.

The follow-up communication is an extension of the crisis recovery phase. Crisis managers maintain a positive organization-stakeholder relationship by keeping stakeholders informed about the crisis even when it is over and by continuing to answer new inquiries. Crisis managers should update the stakeholders on the progress and results of ongoing investigations and the actions taken to prevent a repeat of the crisis. In regards to preventing future crises, crisis managers might tell stakeholders when the changes have been completed or how well the changes are working. The changes actually become a part of the crisis prevention subphase because the actions are designed to prevent future crises. Any crisis must be monitored when it is over, even if no changes are created. Crisis tracking monitors factors that produced the crisis to see if another threat may arise. Crisis tracking feeds back into signal detection and crisis preparation. Simply put, the postcrisis phase ends with crisis managers moving back to the actions involved in the precrisis phase of crisis management; the process is ongoing.

Conclusion

Even when a crisis is perceived to be over, the efforts of the crisis management process remain in motion. The crisis management performance must be evaluated. Careful evaluation is essential to improved crisis management performance. The downside is that a thorough evaluation is time-consuming and somewhat painful. Still, the rewards more than justify the expenditure of resources. Evaluation and crisis documentation should become a part of the functional institutional memory. A well-organized recording of crisis information will allow the information to be used effectively during future crisis management efforts. Lastly, the crisis team must help in any continuing investigations, maintain the flow of follow-up information to stakeholders, and continue to track the crisis. In so doing, the crisis team has a natural segue back to the precrisis phase of crisis management showing that crisis management can be an ongoing process.

9

Final Observations
and Lessons

Developing a comprehensive crisis management program that captures the ongoing nature of crisis management is not an easy task. The crisis management process is varied and requires the integration of knowledge from such diverse areas as small group decision making, media relations, environmental scanning, risk assessment, crisis communication, crisis plan development, evaluation methods, and relationship management. A diverse set of crisis management writings must be navigated to develop a complete crisis management process. Complete means that the program covers every stage and substage of the crisis management process. It is a daunting but necessary task to sort through the plethora of crisis management information. How else can a comprehensive crisis management program be developed?

The primary goal of this book is to offer an integrative framework that simplifies the task of organizing crisis management information. An ongoing approach based on a three-staged model of crisis management provides the foundation. The three stages are precrisis, crisis event, and postcrisis, with each stage being composed of three substages. The stages are used to summarize and organize various insights into the crisis management process. The myriad of ideas from different areas are synthesized into one continuous crisis management process. The end product is a guide for developing each stage in the ongoing crisis management process. The book is a living guide because future developments in crisis management can be easily assimilated into the comprehensive framework of the three-staged approach.

The three-staged model articulated in this book provides a variety of suggestions about "how to do" crisis management. Crisis practitioners, researchers, and educators can benefit from the crisis insights of the numerous crisis experts cited in this volume. As a final statement, I would like to highlight three very valuable lessons. One, crisis management is not a simple collection of various actions relevant only during a training drill or actual crisis. Rather, crisis management is an ongoing process of intricate, interwoven steps. Two, specific knowledge, skills, and traits are associated with effective crisis managers. Selection and training of crisis personnel should seek to maximize those knowledge, skills, and traits. Three, crisis management involves the development and maintenance of procedures designed to improve the flow of information before, during, and after a crisis. Reviewing each of the three lessons reinforces the utility of the continuous crisis management approach to practitioners, researches, and educators.

Crisis Management Is Ongoing

The call for crisis preparedness was the initial message delivered by crisis management advocates. As late as the 1980s, more than 50% of all major organizations had crisis management plans (CMPs), but the number has yet to reach the 60% mark (Guth, 1995). There is a danger in mistaking crisis preparation for crisis management. Some organizations develop an unwarranted sense of security when they have completed their crisis preparation. Having a CMP, crisis team, crisis portfolio, or crisis communication system is but one stage in a larger process. Failure to appreciate the larger process precludes an organization from deriving the complete benefits from a crisis management program.

Furthermore, crisis management must be viewed as a daily effort, not just an "as-needed" concern. Crisis prevention best illustrates the daily nature of crisis management. New information from the crisis-sensing network must be processed and evaluated each day. In addition, current efforts to prevent crises, such as risk reduction, must be implemented and their effects monitored regularly. Even crisis preparation should not be stagnant. Organizations should routinely test and revise the various elements of crisis preparation. Revisions would include updating the CMP, upgrading or teaching new skills to the crisis management team (CMT), reassessing the crisis portfolio, and improving the crisis communication system. Because organizations, their personnel, the environment, and technology change, the elements of crisis preparation also must change. Practice and actual crises provide the data for evaluating crisis management performance. The evaluation guides the revisions to crisis preparation and prevention. Furthermore, the follow-up from an actual crisis segues back to crisis prevention. Crisis management is not a limited resource that is drawn on only during real or simulated crises. Instead, crisis management should be a daily activity performed by a distinct crisis management unit within the organization.

An ongoing approach to crisis management teaches practitioners the necessity of working on crisis management daily. An organization should dedicate some personnel to crisis management on a full-time basis. Although the CMT is valuable operating as an ad hoc unit during a crisis, at least one person must be monitoring the everyday demands of the crisis management process. Researchers can locate their work within the larger framework of the crisis management process. The contextualization helps researchers to develop links between their specific areas of crisis management study and the entire crisis management process. For instance, those studying crisis communication strategies focus on actions taken during the crisis event stage. Researchers can explore more fully how their results might inform either the crisis preparation or crisis evaluation phases. Lessons about crisis communication can enhance the preparation by establishing precrisis communication guidelines and aid in the follow-up communication required during the postcrisis phase. Educators can structure their crisis management teaching around the three stages of the ongoing approach. Students would be taught the value of each stage, the tools necessary to develop each stage, and the importance of integrating the stages.

Knowledge, Skills, and Traits

The selection and training of crisis team members are generally in a rather primitive state. Crisis team selection is based almost exclusively on a person's functional position within an organization. As discussed in Chapter 5, the crisis team membership should reflect key areas in the organization such as operations, public relations, legal, and security (Littlejohn, 1983; Regester, 1989). Team members are trained to execute the CMP, a group-level skill. The spokespersons are selected for their knowledge base or media skills. Spokesperson training emphasizes practice media sessions—being asked questions in a mock press conference. Chapter 5 related the merits and limitations of these practices. The value of improving the current selection and training of crisis teams warrants further attention.

Crisis Teams

The crisis team is critical to the success of the crisis management process. The best CMP and communication systems are of little value when used improperly. A fitting analogy is a state-of-the-art manufacturing facility being operated by ill-trained workers. No matter how good the equipment might be, the actual process and end product quality are poor because the workers do not know how to maximize the value of the equipment. The selection and training of crisis team members must seek to maximize the knowledge, skills, and traits that facilitate group performance. Decision making should be at the heart of the selection and training process. Crisis teams should be equipped for success. Equipment for success includes training on essential knowledge and skills such as decision making, conflict resolution, structuring arguments, listening skills, and managing stress.

Selection is another means by which crisis team performance might be improved. Certain personality traits can help or hinder the functioning of a crisis team. The relevant traits identified in Chapter 5 include low group communication apprehension, a cooperative orientation, high ambiguity tolerance, at least moderate argumentativeness, and low verbal aggressiveness. The value of these traits is a function of the stress, communication demands, and conflict that are natural in a crisis team.

In the ideal world, the crisis team members would be selected through a combination of trait evaluation and functional area. Each functional area would identify a pool of potential candidates for the crisis team. A trait assessment instrument would be given to all potential team members. The people with the most favorable profiles would be selected to represent their functional area on the CMT. Not all selection can be done in this fashion. However, trait assessment is beneficial even when it is not used as grounds for selection.

One benefit of trait assessment is that it provides the crisis team leader(s) with a more complete picture of their team members. A leader can benefit from knowing about the strengths and weaknesses of each team member. For instance, what if the team member from operations has high group communication anxiety? The team leader must work to solicit input from the operations representative. Or, say the team member from legal is high in verbal aggression. The team leader must monitor the legal representative to prevent personal attacks and the destructive use of conflict in the crisis team. A second benefit is that team members have a better understanding of their own strengths and weaknesses. Programs can be developed to help team members cope with limiting traits. The best examples are the programs developed to reduce communication apprehension. There are limits to these programs—do not expect them to produce huge changes in all traits. Still, self-awareness is a powerful tool for people trying to work through their own limitations.

The Spokesperson

The spokesperson is a specialized member of the CMT. The selection and training of spokespersons is in a more advanced state of development than typically is the case for general team selection and training. Spokespersons are chosen in part because they have proven to be effective in dealing with the media. The proof might come from practice or from past actual experiences with the media. However, functional knowledge can be a driving force at times for spokesperson selection. The media may want to question someone with direct knowledge of a particular subject. An environmental crisis demands an environmental expert from the environmental unit, whereas a production accident may require an operations expert from the manufacturing unit. As noted in Chapter 5, an organization must train a number of potential spokespersons for meeting with the media.

It would be unfair to expect training to transform all spokespersons into dynamic, charismatic speakers. Not every one will reach high levels of delivery proficiency. The goal should be to develop a set of core delivery competencies. The core delivery competencies consist of eye contact with the audience at least 60% of the time, minimal use of adaptors/eliminate fidgeting, minimal verbal disfluencies/eliminate repeated disfluencies, varied vocal qualities/avoid monotone, use of hand gestures, and an expressive face. The emphasis is placed on eliminating the negative delivery elements that foster perceptions of deception. Reducing the negative delivery factors will naturally expand the positive delivery factors that build credibility. Not everyone can become a dynamic speaker, but all should be trainable to not look like they are lying.

The knowledge, skills, and traits discussion of crisis team members should help practitioners to develop more effective crisis teams. Specific ideas are provided for improving both the selection and training of crisis team members. These suggestions include screening tests for traits, developing crisis team training procedures, and assessing crisis team performance on a variety of individual-level skills, as well as group-level skills. Combined, the ideas should help to produce crisis teams that are well equipped and trained for the task. The same holds true for spokesperson training. A suggestion offered for expanding the media training is to include more delivery skills.

Researchers can find new avenues of inquiry embedded in the discussion of knowledge, skills, and traits. People have just begun to explore the actual functioning of crisis teams and the effectiveness of crisis spokespersons (e.g., Williams & Olaniran, 1994). The ideas for improving crisis teams and spokespersons are based on the small group and public speaking research. Although the ideas should be applicable, most have yet to be tested.

The knowledge, skills, and trait discussions offer educators specific topics and skills that should be taught to students. For instance, a crisis management course benefits from the inclusion of topics concerning small group decision making and public speaking. The knowledge base for decision making and public speaking would be provided along with opportunities to practice skills and to be evaluated on the performance of small group decision making and delivery.

Crisis Management Procedures

In presenting the ongoing approach, a number of procedures were developed to facilitate the crisis management process. Two procedures deserve to be highlighted: the crisis-sensing network and the stakeholder communication network. These two procedures capture the ideas of crisis management as an ongoing process and the need for integration in crisis management.

Crisis-Sensing Network

The bulk of the crisis management writings focuses on either the CMP (e.g., Katz, 1987) or how to respond to a crisis (e.g., Siomkos & Shrivastava, 1993). Both are critical subject matter that any crisis manger should know. A danger develops as crisis mangers focus on the later stages of the crisis management process and devote insufficient attention to looking for potential crises. A well-rounded crisis management program divides attention equally between the precrisis, crisis event, and postcrisis stages.

The crisis-sensing network operates every day as organizational units scan the environment and internal operations for potential crises. Whether the information is related to developing issues, risk, or relationship problems with stakeholders, crisis managers seek to locate and defuse potential crisis situations. The constant need to scan for crises reinforces the belief that crisis management is a full-time function. Furthermore, the way postcrisis monitoring of a crisis flows back into the crisis-sensing network emphasizes the continuity between the various crisis management stages and substages. The continuous nature of crisis management is revealed in both its daily operation and the connection between its stages.

The crisis-sensing network underscores the need to integrate organizational units. No one organizational unit monitors all the various sources that might reveal a crisis. Diverse information about external political and social issues, production, product safety, transportation, regulatory compliance, insurance risks, and customer complaints are just a part of the crisis-sensing network. To operate effectively, the crisis management unit must receive timely information from all of the other organizational units collecting data relevant to crises. Without the integration of the various scanning mechanisms into the crisis-sensing network, the crisis managers cannot be as effective in crisis detection and prevention as they should be. Integration demands that other organizational units respect and cooperate with those assigned the task of crisis management.

Stakeholder Communication Network

Virtually every CMP includes contact information for reaching various stakeholders. The media contacts are a foregone conclusion (Barton, 1993; Gilmore, 1988; Slahor, 1989). Crisis managers also recognize the value of the other stakeholders such as government officials (Blair, 1987), the community (Benedict, 1994), and the investors and financial community (Pincus, 1986). One function of the stakeholder communication network is to track who from the organization communicates with a particular stakeholder and the channels used to reach the stakeholder. During a crisis, the stakeholder communication network information is used when the organization needs to send messages to specific stakeholders. Once more the organizational units must work as an integrated unit to fulfill the potential of crisis management.

The value of the stakeholder communication network extends beyond how to reach stakeholders. Another part of the network is working on the relationship between the organization and the stakeholder. Working on stakeholder relationships involves all three stages of the crisis management process. Crisis managers should know the precrisis quality of the organization-stakeholder relationship. As detailed in Chapter 4, a favorable precrisis relationship is a great asset to crisis managers. The quality of the postcrisis relationship must also be evaluated. The goal is to prevent the crisis from damaging the relationship. In some cases, exceptional crisis management efforts might even strengthen the bonds between the organization and its stakeholders. The relationship builds around frequent two-way communication between the organization and its stakeholders. Communication includes words and actions. Actions include meeting stakeholder expectations and delivering on promises to stakeholders. An organization should monitor its actions to see if it is meeting key stakeholder expectations and delivering on promises, especially those made during crises. Clearly, maintaining the stakeholder network involves integrating all three stages of the crisis management process and communicating with stakeholders continuously—before, during, and after a crisis.

Value to and of Public Relations Personnel

When we think about public relations and crises, the term *media relations* immediately comes to mind. Crisis management affords people in public relations an opportunity to move beyond media relations and into the dominant coalition—the group in the organization that makes decisions. To be in the dominant coalition, public relations people must demonstrate that they possess certain information that is critical to the operation of the organization (Grunig et al., 1992). Being vital members of the CMT indicates the value of public relations to the dominant coalition. Public relations personnel can be vital because of their roles in the crisis-sensing network and the stakeholder communication network. Part of the public relations person's job is communication with stakeholders. Public relations helps to collect information about any problems with stakeholders—part of the crisis-sensing network. In addition, public relations people are trained to resolve these problems, which helps to build favorable organization-stakeholder relationships—part of maintaining the stakeholder communication network (Grunig & Repper, 1992).

Public relations personnel bring more to the CMT than media relations skills. The public relations person brings important information about stakeholders needed for decision making and is a vital link to stakeholders for monitoring and building relationships. By performing these critical tasks in crisis management, public relations personnel help to establish their value as members of the dominant coalition. Movement into the dominant coalition is highly valued by the field of public relations. The move to the dominant coalition helps to protect the integrity of public relations by preventing encroachment. In turn, the job of the public relations practitioner is more secure and receives higher pay (Kelly, 1994). Crisis management provides an opportunity for public relations personnel to demonstrate their full range of skills and value to the dominant coalition.

Final Thoughts

Throughout this book I have been trying to synthesize existing crisis management ideas with some new ideas to produce a framework for approaching crisis management. The framework was intended to be a tool for integrating the diverse writings and ideas about crisis management into a manageable guide for those interested in crisis management. The end result is something that is not completely new or a restatement of existing works. The crisis management process was divided into three stages as a way to organize and synthesize the various crisis management insights. The basic three-staged model of crisis management emphasizes the ongoing nature of the crisis management process. Crisis management never ends. At any given time, the crisis manager is simply working on different parts of the crisis management process. I believe the integrative power of this book offers unique insights into crisis management. As you have reached the end of the book, you can decide whether it has influenced your views on the crisis management process.

Appendix

Possible Case Studies

Listed below are possible case studies that can be used in the application points. Each crisis lists the organization involved, the year the crisis began, and a brief description of the crisis.

Odwalla, Inc.	1996	*E. coli* poisoning
Dayton Hudson Corp.	1990	Protests over Planned Parenthood grant
Music Television (MTV)	1994	Protests over *Beavis and Butt-head*
Coca-Cola	1990	MagiCan promotion problem
NEC Corp. and Motorola, Inc.	1993	Brain cancer scare
Eli Lilly	1990	Concern over their drug Prozac
Procter & Gamble	1990	Protests over Folgers coffee
Firestone	1978	Problem with tire safety
Gerber	1986	Reports of glass in baby food
General Dynamics	1985	Defense contract fraud
Hudson Food	1997	*E. coli* poisoning
Jack-in-the-Box	1993	*E. coli* poisoning
Kraft USA	1989	Promotional error
Victor Kiam (CEO)	1990	Derogatory remarks
Mitsubishi Motor Manufacturing	1996	Sexual harassment
Nike	1990	PUSH boycott
Nike	1997	Mistreatment of Asian workers

Perrier	1990	Benzene in its water
Reebok	1989	Rumor linking it to South Africa
Suzuki	1988	Samurai rollover problem
Snapple Beverage Corp.	1993	Racism rumors
Texaco	1996	Racial slur
United Way	1992	Inappropriate use of funds
General Motors	1993	C/K pickup lawsuits
Chrysler	1987	Odometer fraud
Waldenbooks	1990	Protests from American Family Association
Sears	1992	Automotive unit fraud
Philip Morris	1989	Protest over sponsorship of the Bill of Rights
R. J. Reynolds	1989	Uptown cigarette said to be racist
Procter & Gamble (Citrus Hill)	1991	FDA action on fresh label
PepsiCo	1993	Syringe scare
PepsiCo	1989	Protest of use of Madonna video in its advertising
Astra USA	1996	Sexual harassment
Taco Bell	1990	Sports bottle giveaway problem
Morrison-Knudsen Corp.	1988	Proposed fines
Occidental Petroleum Corp.	1988	Safety procedures questioned
Avon Products	1988	Boycott by union
Eastern Airlines	1988	Proposed fines
Philip Petroleum Corp.	1989	Explosion
Borden, Inc.	1989	Bad milk
Gerber Products	1989	Problem with toasted oat rings
Amtrak	1989	Crash
McDonald's Corp.	1990	Boycott
Fish Engineering & Construction	1992	Accident investigation
Chrysler	1993	Minivan and National Highway Traffic Safety Administration
Heineken	1993	Glass in beer
Baxter International, Inc.	1993	Arab boycott
Sizzler International, Inc.	1993	*E. coli* poisoning

References

Adams, P. (1996). A state's well-oiled injustice. *World Press Review, 43*(1), 14-15.

Allen, M. W., & Caillouet, R. H. (1994). Legitimation endeavors: Impression management strategies used by an organization in crisis. *Communication Monographs, 61,* 44-62.

Ammerman, D. (1995). What's a nice company like yours doing in a story like this? In L. Barton (Ed.), *New avenues in risk and crisis management* (Vol. 3, pp. 3-8). Las Vegas, NV: UNLV Small Business Development Center.

Annen, P., & McCormick, J. (1997). More than a tune-up: Tough going in a fight against sexual harassment. *Newsweek, 130*(21), 50-52.

Augustine, N. R. (1995). Managing the crisis you tried to prevent. *Harvard Business Review, 73*(6), 147-158.

Balik, S. (1995). Media training: Boot camp for communicator. *Communication World, 12,* 22-25.

Balzer, W. K., & Sulsky, L. M. (1992). Halo and performance appraisal research: A critical examination. *Journal of Applied Psychology, 77*(6), 975-985.

Barge, J. K. (1994). *Leadership: Communication skills for organizations and groups.* New York: St. Martin's.

Baron, R. A. (1983). *Behavior in organizations: Understanding and managing the human side of work.* Boston: Allyn & Bacon.

Barry, R. A. (1984). Crisis communications: What to do when the roof falls in. *Business Marketing, 69,* 96-100.

Barton, L. (1993). *Crisis in organizations: Managing and communicating in the heat of chaos.* Cincinnati, OH: College Divisions South-Western.

159

Barton, L. (1995, August). *Your crisis management plan*. Paper presented at the meeting of New Avenues in Crisis Management, Las Vegas, NV.

Baskin, O., & Aronoff, C. (1988). *Public relations: The profession and the practice* (2nd ed.). Dubuque, IA: William C. Brown.

Baucus, M. S., & Baucus, D. A. (1997). Paying the piper: An empirical examination of longer-term financial consequences of illegal corporate behavior. *Academy of Management Journal, 40*(1), 129-151.

Baucus, M. S., & Near, J. P. (1991). Can illegal corporate behavior be predicted? An event history analysis. *Academy of Management Journal, 34*(1), 9-36.

Bediean, A. G. (1989). *Management* (2nd ed.). Chicago: Dryden.

Benedict, A. C. (1994). After a crisis: Restoring community relations. *Communication World, 11,* 20-24.

Benoit, W. L. (1995). *Accounts, excuses, and apologies: A theory of image restoration.* Albany: State University of New York Press.

Benoit, W. L. (1997). Image repair discourse and crisis communication. *Public Relations Review, 23*(2), 177-180.

Benson, J. A. (1988). Crisis revisted: An analysis of strategies used by Tylenol in the second tampering episode. *Central States Speech Journal, 39,* 49-66.

Berg, D. M., & Robb, S. (1992). Crisis management and the "paradigm case." In E. L. Toth & R. L. Heath (Eds.), *Rhetorical and critical approaches to public relations* (pp. 93-110). Hillsdale, NJ: Lawrence Erlbaum.

Bergman, E. (1994). Crisis? What crisis? *Communication World, 11*(4), 9-13.

Berelson, B. (1952). *Content analysis in communication research.* New York: Free Press.

Billings, R. S., Milburn, T. W., & Schaalman, M. L. (1980). A model of crisis perception: A theoretical and empirical analysis. *Administrative Science Quarterly, 25,* 300-316.

Birch, J. (1994). New factors in crisis planning and response. *Public Relations Quarterly, 39,* 31-34.

Birsch, D., & Fielder, J. H. (1994). *The Ford Pinto case: A study in applied ethics, business, and technology.* Albany: State University of New York Press.

Blair, I. C. (1987). Crisis management. *Beverage World, 106,* 20, 90.

Bobbitt, R. (1995). An Internet primer for public relations. *Public Relations Quarterly, 40,* 27-32.

Boffey, P. M. (1986, February 19). Shuttle head says he was not told of cold readings. *New York Times,* p. A1.

Botan, C. (1993). A human nature approach to image and ethics in international public relation. *Journal of Public Relations Research, 5*(2), 71-82.

Boulding, K. E. (1977). *The image: Knowledge in life and society.* Ann Arbor: University of Michigan Press.

Bradsher, K. (1996, April 26). Ford announces recall of 8.7 million cars and trucks. *New York Times,* p. D1.

Brummett, B. (1980). Towards a theory of silence as a political strategy. *Quarterly Journal of Speech, 66,* 289-303.

Buchholz, R. A. (1990). *Essentials of public policy for management* (2nd ed.). Englewood Cliffs, NJ: Prentice Hall.

Burgoon, J. K., Birk, T., & Pfau, M. (1990). Nonverbal behaviors, persuasion and credibility. *Human Communication Research, 17,* 140-169.

Carney, A., & Jorden, A. (1993). Prepare for business-related crises. *Public Relations Journal, 49,* 34-35.

Caruba, A. (1994). Crisis PR: Most are unprepared. *Occupational Hazards, 56*(9), 85.

Center, A. H., & Jackson, P. (1995). *Public relations practices: Managerial case studies and problems* (5th ed.). Englewood Cliffs, NJ: Prentice Hall.

Chronology of an institutional shareholder campaign (Sears). (1994). *Harvard Business Review, 72,* 142-143.

Clampitt, P. G. (1991). *Communicating for managerial effectiveness.* Newbury Park, CA: Sage.

Clarkson, M. B. E. (1991). Defining, evaluating, and managing corporate social performance: A stakeholder management model. In J. E. Post (Ed.), *Research in corporate social performance and policy* (pp. 331-358). Greenwich, CT: JAI.

Clarkson, M. B. E. (1995). A stakeholder framework for analyzing and evaluating corporate social performance. *Academy of Management Review, 20,* 92-117.

Coates, J. F., Coates, V. T., Jarratt, J., & Heinz, L. (1986). *Issues management: How you can plan, organize, and manage for the future.* Mt. Airy, MD: Lomond.

Cook, D., & Miller, S. (1986, March 17). Why Gerber is standing its ground. *Business Week,* pp. 50-51.

Coombs, W. T. (1992). The failure of the task force on food assistance: A case study of the role of legitimacy in issue management. *Journal of Public Relations Research, 4*(2), 101-122.

Coombs, W. T. (1995a). Choosing the right words: The development of guidelines for the selection of the "appropriate" crisis response strategies. *Management Communication Quarterly, 8,* 447-476.

Coombs, W. T. (1995b, November). *The revised catalytic model: Progression in the evolution of issues management.* Paper presented at the meeting of the Speech Communication Association, San Antonio, TX.

Coombs, W. T. (1996). Alternative resources for public diplomacy: The "net" as a viable resource. In A. F. Alkhafji & J. Biberman (Eds.), *Business research yearbook: Global Perspectives* (Vol. 3, pp. 704-708). Lanham, MD: University Press of America.

Coombs, W. T. (1998). An analytic framework for crisis situations: Better responses from a better understanding of the situation. *Journal of Public Relations Research, 10*(3), 179-193.

Coombs, W. T., & Chandler, R. C. (1996). Crisis teams: Revisiting their selection and training. In L. Barton (Ed.), *New avenues in risk and crisis management* (Vol. 5, pp. 7-15). Las Vegas, NV: UNLV Small Business Development Center.

Coombs, W. T., Hazleton, V., Holladay, S. J., & Chandler, R. C. (1995). The crisis grid: Theory and application in crisis management. In L. Barton (Ed.), *New avenues in risk and crisis management* (Vol. 4, pp. 30-39). Las Vegas, NV: UNLV Small Business Development Center.

Coombs, W. T., & Holladay, S. J. (1996). Communication and attributions in a crisis: An experimental study of crisis communication. *Journal of Public Relations Research, 8*(4), 279-295.

Cooper, R. (1997, Summer). A historical look at the Pepsi/Burma boycott. *The Boycott Quarterly,* pp. 12-15.

Couretas, J. (1985). Preparing for the worst. *Business Marketing, 70,* 96-100.

Crable, R. E., & Vibbert, S. L. (1985). Managing issues and influencing public policy. *Public Relations Review, 11,* 3-16.

Crable, R. E., & Vibbert, S. L. (1986). *Public relations as communication management.* Edina, MN: Bellwether.

Dagnoli, J., & Colford, S. W. (1991, March 18). Brief slump expected for Sudafed. *Advertising Age,* p. 53.

Daniels, T. D., Spiker, B. K., & Papa, M. J. (1997). *Perspectives on organizational communication* (4th ed.). Dubuque, IA: Brown & Benchmark.

Darling, J. R. (1994). Crisis management in international business: Keys to effective decision making. *Leadership & Organizational Development Journal Annual, 15*(8), 3-8.

de Turck, M. A., & Miller, G. R. (1985). Deception and arousal: Isolating the behavioral correlates of deception. *Human Communication Research, 12,* 181-201.

Denbow, C. J., & Culbertson, H. M. (1985). Linking beliefs and diagnosing image. *Public Relations Review, 11,* 29-37.

Dilenschneider, R. L., & Hyde, R. C. (1985). Crisis communications: Planning for the unplanned. *Business Horizons, 28,* 35-38.

Dionisopolous, G. N., & Vibbert, S. L. (1988). CBS vs Mobil Oil: Charges of creative bookkeeping. In H. R. Ryan (Ed.), *Oratorical encounters: Selected studies and sources of 20th century political accusation and apologies* (pp. 214-252). Westport, CT: Greenwood.

Donaldson, T., & Preston, L. E. (1995). The stakeholder theory of the corporation: Concepts, evidence, and implications. *Academy of Management Review, 20,* 65-91.

Donath, B. (1984). Why you need a crisis PR plan. *Business Marketing, 69,* 4.

Dornheim, M. A. (1996). Recovered FMC memory puts new spin on Cali accident. *Aviation Week & Space Technology, 145*(11), 58-62.

Dozier, D. M. (1992). The organizational roles of communications and public relations practitioners. In J. E. Grunig (Ed.), *Excellence in public relations and communication management* (pp. 327-356). Hillsdale, NJ: Lawrence Erlbaum.

Duffy, B., & Beddingfield, K. T. (1996). The sound of silence: More evidence from TWA Flight 800 suggests there was a bomb aboard. *U.S. News & World Report, 121*(5), 28-31.

Dutton, J. E. (1986). The processing of crisis and non-crisis strategic issues. *Journal of Management Studies, 23*(5), 501-517.

Dutton, J. E., & Ashford, S. J. (1993). Selling issues to top management. *Academy of Management Review, 18*(3), 397-428.

Dutton, J. E., & Duncan, R. B. (1987). The creation of momentum for change through the process of strategic issue diagnosis. *Strategic Management Journal, 8,* 279-295.

Dutton, J. E., & Jackson, S. E. (1987). Categorizing strategic issues: Links to organizational action. *Academy of Management Review, 12,* 76-90.

Dutton, J. E., & Ottensmeyer, E. (1987). Strategic issue management systems: Forms, functions, and context. *Academy of Management Review, 12,* 355-365.

Dyer, S. C. (1996). Descriptive modeling for public relations scanning: A practitioner's perspective. *Journal of Public Relations Research, 8*(3), 137-150.

Egelhoff, W. G., & Sen, F. (1992). An information-processing model of crisis management. *Management Communication Quarterly, 5,* 443-484.

Ewing, R. P. (1979). The uses of futurist techniques in issues management. *Public Relations Quarterly, 24*(4), 15-18.

Fahey, A., & Dagnoli, J. (1990, June 18). PM ready to deal with outdoor ad foes. *Advertising Age,* pp. 1, 31.

Fairhurst, G. T., & Sarr, R. A. (1996). *The art of framing: Managing the language of leadership.* San Francisco: Jossey-Bass.

Fearn-Banks, K. (1996). *Crisis communications: A casebook approach.* Mahwah, NJ: Lawrence Erlbaum.

Feeley, T. H., & de Turck, M. A. (1995). Global cue usage in behavioral lie detection. *Communication Quarterly, 43*(4), 420-430.

Finet, D. (1994). Sociopolitical consequences of organizational expression. *Journal of Communication, 44*(4), 114-131.

Fink, S. (1986). *Crisis management: Planning for the inevitable.* New York: AMACOM.

Fink, S., Beak, J., & Taddeo, K. (1971). Organizational crisis and change. *Journal of Applied Behavioral Science, 7,* 15-37.

Fitzpatrick, K. R. (1995). Ten guidelines for reducing legal risks in crisis management. *Public Relations Quarterly, 40*(2), 33-38.

Fitzpatrick, K. R., & Rubin, M. S. (1995). Public relations vs. Legal strategies in organizational crisis decisions. *Public Relations Review, 21*(1), 21-33.

Five missing in chemical plant explosion [Online]. (1998, January 7). Available: Yahoo/ United Press International [January 8, 1998].

Fombrun, C., & Shanley, M. (1990). What's in a name? Reputation building and corporate strategy. *Academy of Management Journal, 33*(2), 233-258.

Four missing in chemical plant explosion [Online]. (1998, January 8). Available: Yahoo/ United Press International [January 8, 1998].

Frank, J. N. (1994). Plan ahead for effective crisis management, expert advises. *Beverage Industry, 85*(4), 22.

Freeman, A. (1996). Sanctioning Burma. *Multinational Monitor, 17*(6), 6.

Gagnon, E. (1994). *What's on the Internet.* Berkeley, CA: Peachpit.

Garvin, A. P. (1996). *The art of being well informed.* Garden City Park, NY: Avery.

Gellene, D. (1993, October 22). New dispute brewing for Snapple. *New York Times,* p. D3.

Gilmore, F. (1988). Dealing with the press in a serious emergency. *Supervision, 49,* 9-11.

Goldhaber, G. M. (1990). *Organizational communication* (5th ed.). Dubuque, IA: William C. Brown.

Goldstein, I. L. (1993). *Training in organizations: Needs assessment, development and evaluation* (3rd ed.). Monterey, CA: Brooks/Cole.

Gonzalez-Herrero, A., & Pratt, C. B. (1995). How to manage a crisis before—or whenever—it hits. *Public Relations Quarterly, 40*(1), 25-29.

Gonzalez-Herrero, A., & Pratt, C. B. (1996). An integrated symmetrical model of crisis-communications management. *Journal of Public Relations Research, 8*(2), 79-106.

Gray, P. (1996). The search for sabotage. *Time, 148*(7), 28-32.

Gross, A. E. (1990). How Popeye's and Reebok confronted product rumors. *Adweek's Marketing Week, 31,* 27, 30.

Grunig, J. E. (1992). Communication, public relations, and effective organizations: An overview of the book. In J. E. Grunig (Ed.), *Excellence in public relations and communication management* (pp. 1-30). Hillsdale, NJ: Lawrence Erlbaum.

Grunig, J. E., & Grunig, L. A. (1992). Models of public relations and communication. In J. E. Grunig (Ed.), *Excellence in public relations and communication management* (pp. 285-326). Hillsdale, NJ: Lawrence Erlbaum.

Grunig, L. A., Grunig, J. E., & Ehling, W. P. (1992). What is an effective organization? In J. E. Grunig (Ed.), *Excellence in public relations and communication management* (pp. 65-90). Hillsdale, NJ: Lawrence Erlbaum.

Grunig, J. E., & Repper, F. C. (1992). Strategic management, publics, and issues. In J. E. Grunig (Ed.), *Excellence in public relations and communication management* (pp. 117-158). Hillsdale, NJ: Lawrence Erlbaum.

Guth, D. W. (1993). Crisis plans in short supply. *Public Relations Journal, 49,* 12.

Guth, D. W. (1995). Organizational crisis experience and public relations roles. *Public Relations Review, 21*(2), 123-136.

Hainsworth, B. E. (1990). Issues management: An overview. *Public Relations Review, 16*(1), 3-5.

Harassment costs Astra $10 million. (1998, February 6). *Pantagraph,* p. C3.

Headache? (1986, February 22). *Economist,* p. 30.

Hearit, K. M. (1994). Apologies and public relations crises at Chrysler, Toshiba, and Volvo. *Public Relations Review, 20*(2), 113-125.

Hearit, K. M. (1996). The use of counter-attack in apologetic public relations crises: The case of General Motors vs. Dateline NBC. *Public Relations Review, 22*(3), 233-248.

Heath, R. L. (1988). Integrating issues management and strategic planning. In R. L. Heath (Ed.), *Strategic issues management* (pp. 99-121). San Francisco: Jossey-Bass.

Heath, R. L. (1990). Corporate issues management: Theoretical underpinnings and research foundations. In J. E. Grunig & L. A. Grunig (Eds.), *Public relations research annual* (Vol. 2, pp. 29-66). Hillsdale, NJ: Lawrence Erlbaum.

Heath, R. L. (1994). *Management of corporate communication: From interpersonal contacts to external affairs.* Hillsdale, NJ: Lawrence Erlbaum.

Heath, R. L. (1997). *Strategic issues management: Organizations and public policy challenges.* Thousand Oaks, CA: Sage.

Heath, R. L., & Cousino, K. R. (1990). Issues management: End of first decade progress report. *Public Relations Review, 16*(1), 6-18.

Heath, R. L., & Nelson, R. A. (1986). *Issues management: Corporate public policy making in an information society.* Beverly Hills, CA: Sage.

Heinberg, P. (1963). Relationships of content and delivery to general effectiveness. *Speech Monographs, 30,* 105-107.

Herbert, B. (1997, March 27). Brutality in Vietnam. *New York Times,* p. A19.

Herbig, P., Milewicz, J., & Golden, J. (1994). A model of reputation building and destruction. *Journal of Business Research, 31,* 23-31.

Hibbard, J. (1997). Shell oil shifts safety data to intranet. *Computerworld, 31*(21), 20-21.

Higbee, A. G. (1992, October). Shortening the crisis lifecycle: Seven rules to live by. *Occupational Hazards, 54,* 137-138.

Hirokawa, R. Y. (1985). Discussion procedures and decision-making performance: A test of a functional perspective. *Human Communication Research, 12,* 203-224.

Hirokawa, R. Y. (1988). Group communication and decision making performance: A continued test of the functional perspective. *Human Communication Research, 14,* 487-515.

Hirokawa, R. Y., & Keyton, J. (1995). Perceived facilitators and inhibitors of effectiveness in organizational work teams. *Management Communication Quarterly, 8*(4), 424-446.

Hirokawa, R. Y., & Rost, K. (1992). Effective group decision making in organizations. *Management Communication Quarterly, 5,* 267-288.

Hobbs, J. D. (1995). Treachery by any other name: A case study of the Toshiba public relations crisis. *Management Communication Quarterly, 8,* 323-346.

Holladay, S. J., & Coombs, W. T. (1994). Speaking of visions and visions being spoken: An exploration of the effects of content and delivery on perceptions of leader charisma. *Management Communication Quarterly, 8*(2), 165-189.

Ice, R. (1991). Corporate publics and rhetorical strategies: The case of Union Carbide's Bhopal crisis. *Management Communication Quarterly, 4,* 341-362.

In a crisis. (1993). *Public Relations Journal, 49,* 10-11.

Irvine, R. B., & Millar, D. P. (1996). Debunking the stereotypes of crisis management: The nature of business crises in the 1990's. In L. Barton (Ed.), *New avenues in risk and crisis management* (Vol. 5, pp. 51-63). Las Vegas, NV: UNLV Small Business Development Center.

Jones, B. L., & Chase, W. H. (1979). Managing public policy issues. *Public Relations Review, 5*(2), 3-23.

Kamer, L. (1996). When the crisis is orchestrated: Corporate campaigns and their origins. In L. Barton (Ed.), *New avenues in risk and crisis management* (Vol. 5, pp. 64-72). Las Vegas, NV: UNLV Small Business Development Center.

Katz, A. R. (1987). 10 steps to complete crisis planning. *Public Relations Journal, 43,* 46-47.

Kaufmann, J. B., Kesner, I. F., & Hazen, T. L. (1994). The myth of full disclosure: A look at organizational communications during crises. *Business Horizons, 37,* 29-39.

Kelly, K. (1990, September 24). Dayton Hudson finds there's no graceful way to flip-flop. *Business Week,* p. 50.

Kelly, K. S. (1994). Fund-raising encroachment and the potential of public relations departments in the nonprofit sector. *Journal of Public Relations Research, 6*(1), 1-22.

Kempner, M. W. (1995). Reputation management: How to handle the media during a crisis. *Risk Management, 42*(3), 43-47.

Kilmann, R. H., & Thomas, K. W. (1975). Interpersonal conflict-handling behaviors as reflection of Jungian personality dimensions. *Psychological Reports, 37,* 971-980.

Kiley, D. (1991, March 11). Sudafed deaths spark a backlash against capsules. *Adweek's Marketing Week,* p. 6.

Koepp, S. (1985, September 16). Placing the blame at E. F. Hutton. *Time,* p. 54.

Komaki, J., Heinzmann, A. T., & Lawson, L. (1980). Effects of training and feedback: Component analysis of a behavioral safety program. *Journal of Applied Psychology, 65,* 261-270.

Kouzes, J. M., & Posner, B. Z. (1993). *Credibility: How leaders gain and lose it, why people demand it.* San Francisco: Jossey-Bass.

Kreps, G. L. (1990). *Organizational communication: Theory and practice* (2nd ed.). New York: Longman.

Larson, C. U. (1989). *Persuasion: Reception and responsibility* (5th ed.). Belmont, CA: Wadsworth.

Lauzen, M. M. (1995). Toward a model of environmental scanning. *Journal of Public Relations Research, 7*(3), 187-204.

Lerbinger, O. (1997). *The crisis manager: Facing risk and responsibility.* Mahwah, NJ: Lawrence Erlbaum.

Leon, M. (1983). Tylenol fights back. *Public Relations Journal, 37,* 10-14.

Levitt, A. M. (1997). *Disaster planning and recovery: A guide for facility professionals.* New York: John Wiley.

Littlejohn, R. F. (1983). *Crisis management: A team approach.* New York: American Management Associations.

Loewendick, B. A. (1993, November). Laying your crisis on the table. *Training & Development,* pp. 15-17.

Lukaszewski, J. E. (1987). Anatomy of a crisis response. *Public Relations Journal, 43,* 45-47.

Mackinnon, P. (1996). When silence isn't golden. *Financial Executive, 12*(4), 45-48.

Magiera, M. (1993, June 21). Pepsi weathers tampering hoaxes: It's textbook case of how to come through a PR crisis. *Advertising Age,* p. 1.

Marconi, J. (1992). *Crisis marketing: When bad things happen to good companies.* Chicago: Probus.

Marcus, A. A., & Goodman, R. S. (1991). Victims and shareholders: The dilemmas of presenting corporate policy during a crisis. *Academy of Management Journal, 34,* 281-305.

Maremont, M. (1996, May 13). Abuse of power: The astonishing tale of sexual harassment at Astra USA. *Business Week,* pp. 86-98.

Maynard, R. (1993, December). Handling a crisis effectively. *Nation's Business,* pp. 54-55.

McCroskey, J. C. (1970). Measures of communication-bound anxiety. *Speech Monographs, 37,* 269-277.

McCroskey, J. C. (1972). The implementation of a large-scale program of systematic desensitization for communication apprehension. *Speech Teacher, 21,* 255-264.

McCroskey, J. C. (1997). *An introduction to rhetorical communication* (7th ed.). Boston: Allyn & Bacon.

McGraw, D. (1996). Human error and a human tragedy: The aftermath of the American Airlines crash. *U.S. News & World Report, 120*(1), 38.

Mecham, M. (1986, February 19). Shuttle probe gets testy: Who knew about the cold and when? *USA Today,* p. 1A.

Milas, G. H. (1996). Guidelines for organizing TQM teams. *IIE Solutions, 28*(2), 36-39.

Mitchell, R. K., Agle, R. A., & Wood, D. J. (1997). Toward a theory of stakeholder identification and salience: Defining the principle of who and what really counts. *Academy of Management Review, 22*(4), 853-886.

Mitchell, T. H. (1986). Coping with a corporate crisis. *Canadian Business Review, 13,* 17-20.

Mitroff, I. I. (1986). Teaching corporate America to think about crisis prevention. *Journal of Business Strategy, 6,* 40-47.

Mitroff, I. I. (1988). Crisis management: Cutting through the confusion. *Sloan Management Review, 29,* 15-20.

Mitroff, I. I. (1994). Crisis management and environmentalism: A natural fit. *California Management Review, 36*(2), 101-113.

Mitroff, I. I., Harrington, K., & Gai, E. (1996). Thinking about the unthinkable. *Across the Board, 33*(8), 44-48.

Mitroff, I. I., & McWinney, W. (1987). Disaster by design and how to avoid it. *Training, 24,* 33-34, 37-38.

Mohr, B. (1994, March). The Pepsi challenge: Managing a crisis. *Prepared Foods,* pp. 13-14.

Moore, R. H. (1979). Research by the Conference Board sheds light on problems of semantics, issue identification and classification—and some likely issues for the '80s. *Public Relations Journal, 35,* 43-46.

Moriarity, S. E. (1994). PR and IMC: The benefits of integration. *Public Relations Quarterly, 39*(3), 38-45.

"Muslim Concerns," Nike Press Release, June 24, 1997.

Myers, K. N. (1993). *Total contingency planning for disasters: Managing risk, minimizing loss, ensuring business continuity.* New York: John Wiley.

National Research Council. (1996). *Computing and communications in the extreme: Research for crisis management and application.* Washington, DC: National Academy Press.

"Nearly 200," Odwalla Press Release, October 31, 1996.

Nelkin, D. (1988). Risk reporting and the management of industrial crises. *Journal of Management Studies, 25,* 341-351.

Nevada explosion kills three, injures eight [Online]. (1998, January 7). Available: Yahoo/Reuters [January 8, 1998].

Newsom, D., Turk, J., & Kruckeberg, D. (1996). *This is PR: The realities of public relations* (6th ed.). Belmont, CA: Wadsworth.

Nicholas, R. (1995, November 23). Know comment. *Marketing,* pp. 41-43.

Nisbett, R. E., & Wilson, T. D. (1977). The halo effect: Evidence for unconscious alteration of judgments. *Journal of Personality and Social Psychology, 35*(4), 250-256.

Norton, R. W. (1983). *Communicator style: Theory, applications, and measures.* Beverly Hills, CA: Sage.

O'Connor, M. F. (1985). Methodology for corporate crisis decision-making. In S. J. Andriole (Ed.), *Corporate crisis management* (pp. 239-258). Princeton, NJ: Petrocelli.

O'Hair, D., Friedrich, G. W., Wiemann, J. M., & Wiemann, M. O. (1995). *Competent communication.* New York: St. Martin's.

Orru, M., Biggart, N. W., & Hamilton, G. G. (1991). Organizational isomorphism in East Asia. In W. W. Powell & P. J. DiMaggio (Eds.), *The new institutionalism in organizational analysis* (pp. 361-389). Chicago: University of Chicago Press.

Pace, R. W., & Boren, R. (1973). *The human transaction.* Glenview, IL: Scott, Foresman.

Pauchant, T. C., & Mitroff, I. I. (1992). *Transforming the crisis-prone organization: Preventing individual, organizational, and environmental tragedies.* San Francisco: Jossey-Bass.

Paul, R., & Elder, L. (1995). *An educator's guide to critical thinking terms and concepts* [Online]. Available: http://www.sonoma.edu/cthink/.

Pearson, C. M., & Clair, J. A. (1998). Reframing crisis management. *Academy of Management Review, 23*(1), 59-76.

Pearson, C. M., & Mitroff, I. I. (1993). From crisis prone to crisis prepared: A framework for crisis management. *The Executive, 7*(1), 48-59.

Peters, T. (1994). *The Tom Peters seminar: Crazy times call for crazy organizations.* New York: Vintage.

Pincus, T. H. (1986). A crisis parachute: Helping stock prices have a soft landing. *Journal of Business Strategy, 6,* 32-38.

Pines, W. L. (1985). How to handle a PR crisis: Five dos and five don'ts. *Public Relations Quarterly, 30*(2), 16-19.

Putnam, L. L., & Poole, M. S. (1987). Conflict and negotiation. In F. M. Jablin, L. L. Putnam, K. H. Roberts, & L. W. Porter (Eds.), *Handbook of organizational communication: An interdisciplinary perspective* (pp. 549-599). Newbury Park, CA: Sage.

Putnam, T. (1993, Spring). Boycotts are busting out all over. *Business and Society Review,* pp. 47-51.

Rancer, A. S., Baukus, R. A., & Infante, D. A. (1985). Relations between argumentativeness and belief structures about arguing. *Communication Education, 34,* 37-47.

Redding, W. C. (1972). *Communication within the organization.* Lafayette, IN: Purdue Research Foundation.

Reeves, M. (1996). Weaving a web at the office: Intranets are all the rage in networking technology. *Black Enterprise, 27*(4), 39-41.

Regester, M. (1989). *Crisis management: How to turn a crisis into an opportunity.* London: Hutchinson Business.

Rowley, T. J. (1997). Moving beyond dyadic ties: A network theory of stakeholder influence. *Academy of Management Review, 22*(4), 887-910.

Rupp, D. (1996). Tech versus touch. *HR Focus, 73*(11), 16-18.

Ryan, C. (1991). *Prime time activism: Media strategies for grassroots organizing.* Boston: South End.

Sanger, D. E. (1986, February 28). Communications channels at NASA: Warnings that faded along the way. *New York Times,* p. A13.

Savage, G. T., Nix, T. W., Whitehead, C. J., & Blair, J. D. (1991). Strategies for assessing and managing organizational stakeholders. *The Executive, 5*(2), 61-75.

Scriven, M., & Paul, R. (1996). *Defining critical thinking* [Online]. Available: http:// www.sonoma.edu/cthink/.

Seitel, F. P. (1983). 10 myths of handling bad news. *Bank Marketing, 15,* 12-14.

Sen, F., & Egelhoff, W. G. (1991). Six years and counting: Leaning from crisis management at Bhopal. *Public Relations Review, 17*(1), 69-83.

Sewell, D. (1997, August 13). Small businesses real from strike [Online]. Available: AOL news/The Associated Press [1997, June 14].

Shrivastava, P. (1993). Crisis theory/practice: Towards a sustainable future. *Industrial and Environmental Crisis Quarterly, 7,* 23-42.

Shrivastava, P., & Mitroff, I. I. (1987). Strategic management of corporate crises. *Columbia Journal of World Business, 22,* 5-11.

Siomkos, G., & Shrivastava, P. (1993). Responding to product liability crises. *Long Range Planning, 26*(5), 72-79.

Slahor, S. (1989). Media relations during a crisis. *Supervision, 50,* 9-11.

Smallwood, C. (1995). Risk and organisational behavior: Toward a theoretical framework. In L. Barton (Ed.), *New avenues in risk and crisis management* (Vol. 4, pp. 139-148). Las Vegas, NV: UNLV Small Business Development Center.

Smith, E. B. (1998, January 13). The Zilog mystery: What made so many workers so sick? *USA Today,* pp. B1-B3.

Smith, C. A. P., & Hayne, S. C. (1997). Decision making under time pressure: An investigation of decision speed and decision quality of computer-supported groups. *Management Communication Quarterly, 11*(1), 97-126.

Snyder, A. (1991, April 8). Do boycotts work? *Adweek's Marketing Week,* pp. 16-18.

Snyder, L. (1983). An anniversary review and critique: The Tylenol crisis. *Public Relations Review, 9,* 24-34.

Sonnenfeld, S. (1994). Media policy—What media policy? *Harvard Business Review, 72*(4), 18-19.

Soper, R. H. (1995, August). *Crisis management strategy plan formulation and implementation.* Paper presented at the meeting of New Avenues in Crisis Management, Las Vegas, NV.

Star, M. G. (1993). Sears resolution gains support. *Pension & Investments, 21,* 2.

Stewart, C. J., & Cash, W. B., Jr. (1997). *Interviewing: Principles and practices* (8th ed.). Dubuque, IA: William C. Brown.

Stohl, C., & Coombs, W. T. (1988). Cooperation or cooptation: An analysis of quality circle training manuals. *Management Communication Quarterly, 2,* 63-89.

Stohl, C., & Redding, W. C. (1987). Messages and message exchange processes. In F. M. Jabling, L. L. Putnam, K. H. Roberts, & L. W. Porter (Eds.), *Handbook of organizational communication: An interdisciplinary perspective* (pp. 451-502). Beverly Hills, CA: Sage.

Strauss, G. (1998, January 13). Embezzlement growth is "dramatic." *USA Today,* pp. 1A-2A.

Strnad, P. (1986, March 10). Gerber ignores Tylenol textbook. *Advertising Age, 57,* 3.

Sturges, D. L. (1994). Communicating through crisis: A strategy for organizational survival. *Management Communication Quarterly, 7*(3), 297-316.

Sullivan, M. (1990). Measuring image spillover in umbrella-branded products. *Journal of Business, 63*(3), 309-329.

Tan, A. S. (1985). *Mass communication theories and research.* New York: John Wiley.

Tesser, A., & Rosen, S. (1975). The reluctance to transmit bad news. In L. Berkowitz (Ed.), *Advances in experimental social psychology* (Vol. 8, pp. 193-232). New York: Academic Press.

Thomsen, S. R. (1995). Using online databases in corporate issues management. *Public Relations Review, 21*(2), 103-123.

Trahan, J. V., III. (1993). Media relations in the eye of the storm. *Public Relations Quarterly, 38*(2), 31-33.

Tsui, J. (1993). Tolerance for ambiguity, uncertainty audit qualification and bankers' perceptions. *Psychological Reports, 72,* 915-919.

Turban, D. B., & Greening, D. W. (1997). Corporate social performance and organizational attractiveness to prospective employees. *Academy of Management Journal, 40*(3), 658-672.

Twardy, S. A. (1994). Attorneys and public relations professionals must work hand-in-hand when responding to an environmental investigation. *Public Relations Quarterly, 39*(2), 15-16.

Tyler, L. (1997). Liability means never being able to say you're sorry: Corporate guilt, legal constraints, and defensiveness in corporate communication. *Management Communication Quarterly, 11*(1), 51-73.

Versical, D. (1987, May). An anatomy: Dealers, critics review Audi's crises management. *Automotive News,* p. 1.

Walsh, B. (1995). Beware of the crisis lovers. *Forbes, 155*(12), A17-A18.

Ware, B. L., & Linkugel, W. A. (1973). They spoke in defense of themselves: On the generic criticism of apologia. *Quarterly Journal of Speech, 59,* 273-283.

Watson, R. (1996). Next, a "Eureka" piece. *Newsweek, 128*(10), 48-50.

Weick, K. E. (1979). *The social psychology of organizing* (2nd ed.). Reading, MA: Addison-Wesley.

Weick, K. E. (1988). Enacted sense making in crisis situations. *Journal of Management Studies, 25*(4), 305-317.

Weinstein, S. (1993, August). The hoax that failed. *Progressive Grocer,* p. 17.

Wilcox, D. L., Ault, P. H., & Agee, W. K. (1995). *Public relations: Strategies and tactics* (4th ed). New York: HarperCollins.

Williams, D. E., & Olaniran, B. A. (1994). Exxon's decision-making flaws: The hypervigilant response to the Valdez grounding. *Public Relations Review, 20*(1), 5-18.

Wilsenbilt, J. Z. (1989, Spring). Crisis management planning among U.S. corporations: empirical evidence and a proposed framework. *SAM Advanced Management Journal,* pp. 31-41.

Wilson, S., & Patterson, B. (1987). When the news hits the fan. *Business Marketing, 72,* 92-94.

Wolpin, S. (1995, November). FAQ. *The Rolling Stone Computer Issue,* pp. 24-25.

Wood, D. J. (1991). Corporate social performance revisited. *Academy of Management Review, 16,* 691-718.

Woodcock, C. (1994, November 24). How to face crises with confidence. *Marketing,* pp. 8-10.

Zinn, L., & Regan, M. B. (1993, July 5). The right moves baby. *Business Week,* p. 31.

Index

About the Author

W. Timothy Coombs is Associate Professor in the Department of Communication at Clemson University, where he teaches public relations and crisis management. His doctorate (Purdue University) is in issues management and public affairs. He is a part-time consultant working through Cassandra Communication, an organization specializing in crisis management and communication. In addition to crisis management, he has research interests in international public relations, workplace violence, and Internet applications to politics and public relations. He has published in the *Journal of Public Relations Research, Management Communication Quarterly,* and *Public Relations Review.* This book is a culmination of 7 years of crisis management research and even more years of experience with crises.